Top Notes

T0360051

Selected Poems:
Denise Levertov

Study notes for Extension English
Module B 2015–2020 HSC

Eleni Tatsis & Joanna House

A
FIVE SENSES
PUBLICATION

Five Senses Education Pty Ltd
2/195 Prospect Highway
Seven Hills 2147
New South Wales
Australia

Tatsis, Eleni & House, Joanna
Top Notes – Denise Levertov
ISBN 978 -1- 76032 –106 – 2

2016.09.16

CONTENTS

TOP NOTES SERIES

This series has been created to assist H.S.C. students of English in their understanding of set texts. Top Notes are easy to read, providing analysis of issues and discussion of important ideas contained in the texts.

Particular care has been taken to ensure that students are able to examine each text in the context of the module it has been allocated to.

Each text generally includes:

- Notes on the specific module
- Plot summary
- Character analysis
- Setting
- Thematic concerns
- Language studies
- Essay questions and a modelled response
- Other textual material
- Study practice questions
- Useful quotes

I am sure you will find these Top Notes useful in your studies of English.

Bruce Pattinson
Series Editor

STUDYING EXTENSION ONE

This is a brief analysis of the Extension One course to ensure you are completely familiar with the HSC requirements. If uncertain, check with your teacher or the Board of Studies. Extension English is designed for adept English students. It is challenging and designed to develop your understanding and appreciation of texts, contexts and values. The course allows you to study a specific area of English.

To study Extension English you must be studying the Advanced course in English. In Year 11 you will have studied the Preliminary Extension course. This prepares you for HSC Extension. In your HSC year there are two Extension HSC courses. Extension One is the third unit of study. Extension Two is the fourth unit of study and involves creating an extended composition. You might be doing both courses.

Extension One

- This course involves the study of a module. There are internal choices within each module and choices of texts. As well as school assessment, this course has an external examination. An extended critical and creative response is expected/

- Depending on the Module and the elective chosen, you may have to study two or three prescribed texts. No matter which elective is chosen, students are also expected to select texts of their own choosing, related to the elective.

> **Preliminary Extension Module: Texts, Culture and Value**

↓

> ## HSC Extension Course 1
>
> **Module A – Genre**
> - Life Writing, OR
> - Comedy, OR
> - Science Fiction
>
> OR
>
> **Module B – Texts and Ways of Thinking**
> - After the Bomb, OR
> - Romanticism, OR
> - Navigating the Global
>
> OR
>
> **Module C – Language and Values**
> - Textual Dynamics, OR
> - Language and Gender

> You do *either* Module A, B *or* C. In each module there are three elective choices. You only do ONE. So out of the nine choices in this box you will only study one but you will become an expert in it.

MODULE B: TEXTS AND WAYS OF THINKING
What is meant by Texts and Ways of Thinking?

This module requires students to study texts from a particular historical period and to look at the common ways of thinking for that time. What did people value? What did they think they should value and why? What did people expect from one another? What did people expect from themselves. What was it that they desired? What was it that they held in high esteem? What did people try to achieve and why? How did the social and cultural values help people find happiness or how did those social and cultural values stifle and oppress people's individuality?

The module asks responders to question these ways of thinking. We may view some as positive and others as negative and the authors of the texts may indeed side with one particular way of thinking or they may be extremely critical of these ways of thinking and use their writing as a way to share their ideas. These authors may be writing their texts in order to challenge the predominant ways of thinking of the time and make their audiences see that we need to change our ways in order for humanity to progress in a beneficial way. Conversely, these authors may be writing their texts in order to espouse certain ways of thinking and to promote them to an audience.

Paradigms and Values

The paradigms set out by the rubric are economic, scientific, philosophical and religious. Paradigms are a typical example, pattern or model of something – a way of thinking, set of principles, values or mind-set. In this study, such models apply to ways of thinking and influence our behaviour and society.

For example, in an economic paradigm, wealth is highly valued. The paradigm influences the set of values held by the individual and causes them to judge others or events through a particular lens. A religious paradigm would dominate an individual's way of perceiving the world in a very different manner to an individual operating within a scientific paradigm. For example, the belief of Creationism may conflict with the belief in Darwinism in an 19th Century setting, thus influencing the way responders view the world. A philosophical paradigm encourages the thinker or responder to analyse the world and to question existing metanarratives. The individual who operates within a scientific paradigm is more concerned, today, with advances in technology such as medicine, communication and weapons of warfare.

Values and ways of thinking can be limiting or liberating for the individual when operating within paradigms. The texts studied in this unit will offer a conflict or fusion of these paradigms. In our post modern world, truth becomes uncertain, and perspectives may depend on which paradigm or paradigms are being used to view the world. As Stephen Bonnycastle stated, 'we cannot expect someone working in a different paradigm to agree with our knowledge...we are always influenced by our own paradigms, which in turn, influence our way of thinking'. Further, he claims, 'paradigms are social constructions, like natural languages. Recognising the importance of shared paradigms and valuing the communication that can occur when a paradigm is shared, can give you a new respect for communities and a willingness to tolerate the restrictions they impose.' So we must be aware of what paradigms are operating in any given text and context and be able to highlight how each composer reveals particular values working within their own paradigms.

Paradigms in Levertov's Poetry

'What Were They Like?'

In this poem, Levertov presents a conflict between **economic** and **scientific** paradigms versus **religious** and **philosophical**. The explicit references to warfare and bombing highlight the danger of utilising these damaging ways of thinking which do not allow for the preservation and respect of a people's culture. This contrasts with the religious and philosophical paradigms that Levertov presented, as being callously obliterated, resulting in a loss of culture and tradition.

'The Sun Going Down upon Our Wrath',

This poem's paradigms are quite similar to 'What Were They Like'. Levertov utilises **philosophical** and **religious** ways of thinking to try to convince her audience to abandon their destructive **scientific** and **economic** ways of thinking in light of the institutional thinking of the Vietnam War, environmental degradation and anti-nuclear protesting.

'The Malice of Innocence'

Levertov reflects on a time in her youth when **scientific** and **economic** paradigms were more highly valued than **religious** and **philosophical** paradigms. She realises at an older age, that she sacrificed her humanity and compassion in order to succeed at her work. The mechanical and routine are often privileged over the more abstract emotions, as it is simpler to ignore one's humanity.

'A Place of Kindness'

This poem explores **philosophical** paradigms; it asks the readers to question the burden of knowledge versus the bliss of ignorance. Levertov believes that as a consequence of education and knowledge, corruption is inevitable.

'The Life of Others'

Levertov outlines the limitations of certain paradigms, such as the **economic**, and explores how they constrict our individual and collective humanity. She promotes a **philosophical** paradigm in order to challenge mankind's current ways of thinking.

'What It Could Be'

The poem explores **scientific** and **economic** paradigms, such as uranium mining and critiques institutionalised ways of thinking and their ability to destroy the environment and annihilate humanity.

'Talk in the Dark'

The destructive effects of **scientific** and **economic** paradigms, when dealing with war, are explored in the poem. Levertov utilises **philosophical** paradigms in the form of questioning our existence in order to change the ways of thinking of her audience.

WHAT DO WE MEAN BY NAVIGATING THE GLOBAL?

What is it to navigate?

The word 'navigate' originates from the Latin *navigatus*; *navis* translating as 'ship' and *igare* translating as 'drive'. Thus, the title of the course refers to the way that we individually and collectively drive, steer and hence manage our lives in a global world.

Each of the texts set for study explores ways in which individuals manage their lives in a global world. Some manage to navigate successfully whilst others are challenged by it or simply shy away from it. In each instance it can lead to positive and negative outcomes for the individual.

Each of the texts also shows us the ways in which composers feel we should navigate our lives so that we may lead a fulfilling and purposeful existence which benefits humanity's future.

What is globalisation?

Dictionary.com defines globalisation as *'worldwide integration and development.'*

Whilst the term globalisation came into common use in the 1980s as the result of the emergence of a single world market dominated by multinational companies, the idea stretches back centuries to ancient times, when the Ancient Greeks opened up their doors to trade. An increase in trade between countries throughout the centuries and the consequent social, cultural and technological exchange that has occurred has been viewed both positively and negatively in terms of its impact on traditional culture and values.

Globalisation affects the: economy, environment, culture, society, technology and politics.

Economy

Globalisation has been predominantly a capitalist movement. It has seen the development of multinational companies and international trade and has contributed to an increase in the production of goods and services for profit.

Environment

Climate change, water and air pollution, deforestation and over fishing have all been linked with globalisation.

Culture

Internet, popular culture and international travelling have all impacted culture. Globalisation has been linked to the hybridisation and/or homogenisation of culture.

Society

People living together in community has brought about advances in living standards, health and education.

Technology

The rapid rise of technology has increased the inter connectedness and interdependence of people and countries and has allowed people, worldwide, to share knowledge, paradigms and values.

Politics

Institutions such as the European Union, United Nations, UNICEF, International Criminal Court, The World Trade Organisation and the G8 have seen the reduction of the impact of national states and recognition of global perspectives.

Arguments for and against globalisation

Against globalisation

One of the main criticisms against globalisation is the loss of cultural and traditional values as well as the loss of national identity and language that comes along with being exposed to, as well as adopting, other countries' paradigms-whether by choice or by force or by a slow process of transformation. Another criticism involves the loss of individuality and the emerging prevalence of standardisation that comes as a result of being exposed to the same ideas on a worldwide global scale.

Globalisation has also created inequality. The economic gap between the rich and the poor continues to increase, whilst unemployment in many countries has risen due to outsourcing work to other countries that can perform the job at a reduced cost. It can also involve the exploitation of workers in poorer countries who have to work for longer hours and whose health and safety is not a priority. It can also mean the exploitation of child and prison labour.

Globalisation has also seen an increase in environmental degradation where money, power and political control are valued over the natural environment. Often transnational companies want to place their pollution inducing industries in countries who do not have the resources to control their environment.

Globalisation has also led to a change in values. The pressure to look attractive, to be ambitious, to succeed, to make money, to have the latest technology, to be seen having a good time, has created a society which values appearance over substance. It has also led to other negative traits such as individual greed, dishonesty, competition, aggression, commodification, monopolies, a need to be validated and a sense of entitlement.

For globalisation

On the other-hand, globalisation has had positive effects. The erasure of boundaries of time and space has promoted the experience of different cultures and values and allowed for differences to be celebrated. Technology has allowed for increased communication with the world and this has led to benefits in the fields of education, medicine and science. We are more aware than ever of human rights issues and breaking news across the globe. This has allowed for help on a global scale when disasters have struck or when aid has been needed. Globalisation has brought with it individual freedom, opportunity and choice. It has also erased sources of division such as tribalism and religious fundamentalism as a result of the integration of cultures.

The positive values developed as a result of globalisation include; tolerance, understanding, acceptance, appreciation, charity, giving, sharing, empathy and open-mindedness

Module B: Texts and Ways of Thinking

Before looking more closely at the elective, here is a final reminder of the module. Keep module and elective in mind when you respond to every question.

This module requires students to explore and evaluate a selection of texts relating to a particular historical period. It develops their understanding of the ways in which scientific, religious, philosophical or economic paradigms have shaped and are reflected in literature and other texts. (Refer to the *English Stage 6 Syllabus*, pp 82–83.)

ELECTIVE THREE: NAVIGATING THE GLOBAL. HISTORY AND THEORY

In this elective, students explore and evaluate texts that examine and represent the ideas, impacts and consequences of globalisation. Since the late 20th century, the movement towards a global culture has blurred traditional concepts and boundaries of time and space. Knowledge, values and ways of thinking have become at once global and local through the impact of new technologies and modes of communication. Context, circumstance and perspective have shaped a range of individual and community responses to this changing reality: while some have embraced or reluctantly accepted it, others have challenged or retreated from it. The ideas, language forms, features and structures of texts may reflect or challenge ways of thinking during this period.

In this elective, students are required to study **at least three** of the prescribed texts (including at least two print texts), as well as other related texts of their own choosing. In their responding and composing, they explore, analyse, experiment with and critically evaluate their prescribed texts and a range of other appropriate texts.

Texts can be drawn from a range of times, contexts and media and should reflect the relationships between the global and the local and the significance of these relationships to the life of the individual and their community.

How does the Rubric relate to Levertov's poetry?

There are seven Denise Levertov poems set for study. They include:

- 'What Were They Like?' From *Poems 1960–1967*
  © 1966 by Denise Levertov

- 'The Sun Going Down upon Our Wrath', From *Poems 1968–1972*
  ©1972 by Denise Levertov

- 'The Malice of Innocence', From *Poems 1968–1972*
  ©1972 by Denise Levertov

- 'A Place of Kindness', From *The Freeing of the Dust*
  ©1975 by Denise Levertov

- 'The Life of Others', From *Poems 1972–1982*
  ©1978 by Denise Levertov

- 'What It Could Be', From *Poems 1972–1982*
  ©1975 by Denise Levertov

- 'Talk in the Dark' From *Candles in Babylon*
  ©1982 by Denise Levertov

The rubric requires students to explore the ways of thinking evident in each poem set for study. The historical period for these particular poems encompasses the late 1960s, 1970s and early 1980s. Within these decades there was certainly a change in the ways that people thought. These decades were indeed a time when people challenged the paradigms of their social and cultural contexts. People began to protest about events and decisions they did not agree with.

These events and decisions included:

- institutional thinking,

- the Vietnam War,

- environmental degradation,

- anti-nuclear protesting.

Levertov directly addresses these issues. She protests against them through her poetry and challenges responders. She then asks her audience to reimagine their world without these issues in order to transform their own society and, as a consequence, humanity at large.

Theorists

It is advised that students read widely to develop their knowledge of post modern theory and read theorists of the late 20th and 21st centuries. Suggested theorists are listed below but there are many more, and students are encouraged to undertake further independent investigation in order to produce a thorough, original response.

- Frederic Jameson

- Vaclav Havel

- Jean Baudrillard

- Francis Lyotard

ADDITIONAL HELP WITH NAVIGATING THE GLOBAL: HISTORY AND THEORY

David Strange and Derek Patulny

What is globalisation?

In order to discuss globalisation with any sort of accuracy and depth, many disciplines, some of which you may study – economics, history, design and technology, science, politics and linguistics, should be considered. What does the term, globalisation, describe in a denotative sense? What did Theodore Levitt mean when he coined the word in a Harvard Business School paper back in 1983? Why has it become, in some circles, a derogatory word? Why does the word have such negative, values-linked connotations within an economic paradigm?

How is globalisation commonly understood?

The global world has become synonymous with capitalism, greed, expediency, speed, vulgarity, indulgence, callousness, loneliness, fast-paced knowledge and technology, an ironic sense of detachment from ourselves and others and a lack of purpose. Globalisation might be represented as a painting of a creeping, ugly mass of people consumed with the pursuits of materialism.

To what extent do we value an idea or a corporation because it lays claim to having a 'global' influence? Is this homogeny of ideas detrimental to our sense of the truth? The underlying dilemma of defining the effects of globalisation becomes apparent if we ask ourselves a litany of rhetorical questions focused on the depth and complexity of the problem.

Is globalisation a democratic force? Or is it largely undemocratic in nature? Is the spread of liberal democracy (Westminster parliamentary democracy) ushering in capitalism and globalisation through the back door?

What are the precedents of modern globalisation? Is Christianity the only legitimate example of an early global spread? Was trade in the Roman Empire and even earlier empires a similar example? Does Edward Gibbon's analysis offer us a model for how globalisation will eventually implode? Was it with the invention of the printing press, the industrial revolution and the spread of a lingua franca (English) that we saw the first rise of globalisation?

Later, the ease of travel, spread of the photographic image, radio, television and the internet had a lasting impact upon the isolation and mystery of local communities.

How is globalisation arrested? How do we turn it back? Or are individuals and communities best to initially embrace it only then to reject it in their own time? Or do we openly fight globalisation? If so, how could we openly fight it? Should we jealously cling to our local languages, folk lore, art work, ancient religions, sacred sites and esoteric texts to fight the insidious spread of a world culture? Or, is the better response to seek a world culture through identifying similarities between seemingly disparate cultures? Paradoxically, should global technologies be harnessed to promote the local?

Globalisation, ironically, might save local communities and preserve local folk lore and traditions. Is globalisation another name for 'world consciousness'? Local languages, legends and folklore are now less likely to be lost since the advent of global technologies (tape recorders, cameras, mobile phones and apps) and the focus on indigenous cultures through university departments.

Does the advent of global technology and the increasing awareness of obscure foreign cultures ironically mean that, as individuals, we know more about others and therefore can finally observe Socrates' maxim to *know ourselves?* Does the 'global' world in fact offer us a better perspective on ourselves as individuals?

What is the rubric of Navigating the Global?

In the late 20th century and early 21st century, the move towards a global culture has blurred traditional concepts and boundaries of time and space. Knowledge, values and culture have become at once global and local through the globalisation of communication. Choice and circumstance have created a range of individual and community responses to this changing reality: all must navigate their way and establish their own response to the effects of globalisation. The ideas, language forms, features and structures of texts may reflect or challenge ways of thinking relating to this era.

In this elective students are required to study at least **three of the prescribed texts**, two of which must be print texts, as well as other texts of their own choosing. In responding and composing students explore, analyse, experiment with and critically evaluate their prescribed texts and a range of other appropriate examples. Texts should be drawn from a range of contexts and media and should reflect the relationships between the global and the local and the significance of these relationships to the life of the individual and their community.

Common misconceptions in unit

Student: I went looking for NTG on the internet last night. I only found Board of Studies references.

Teacher: It's a concept. The whole notion is framed around –

Student: Sure it's a concept. It's a made-up concept! It's not a real term. No-one else talks about it. There's no websites that deal with it besides the Board of Studies and Bored of Studies.

Teacher: That's right. It's all about –

Student: You don't understand. It's not a *real* concept like post-modernism. There are hundreds of websites on post-modernism. We could easily research that. There's absolutely nothing on NTG!

Teacher: NTG is an excellent elective for the very reason that what underlies it is a concept demanding a range of interpretations. Cultural contexts as diverse as those found in the relatively modern texts – *The White Tiger*, *Journey to the Stone Country*, Coppola's *Lost in Translation*, Reeve's *Tropic of Cancer* and Levertov's poetry can all be evaluated in terms of paradigms and paradigm shifts. Remember, texts that used to be on this elective can be excellent related texts. For example, Explore Proulx's *The Shipping News,* Theroux's *The Mosquito Coast* and Alastair MacLeod's collection of short stories titled, *Island*. A Five Sense Nexus Related Text Guide is forthcoming for *Island*.

Thinking is the new black

There is seemingly a band of students who undertake Extension each year and who forget that what they have chosen, is in essence, a research course. The 'higher order' thinking required calls for risk, experimentation and debate. For students of English Extension One, far more than for those studying 2 Unit Advanced, teachers are not a concierge to be relied upon to provide conceptual room service. As in: *Knock, knock. Sorry to disturb you sir, but I have your NTG definition as ordered. Where would you like it?*

Extension One rubrics deal with concepts, paradigms and paradoxical ideas, not strictly defined terminologies. Such students seem to think it unfortunate that we do not provide them at the beginning of the course with the formula:

Common errors in the student approach to NTG:

i. Students often believe they need to cite the terms 'local' and 'global' in each and every paragraph of their practice essays. The terms 'local' and 'global' are best employed as adjectives, not abstract nouns. As in, 'The local customs and rituals of the island are compromised by the intrusion of global economic forces.'

ii. Some students attempt to ascribe every character (or animal) in a given text to a notion of 'local' or 'global' – not only is this unnecessary, it erroneously presumes there is a literal truth to the matter. Students at this level ought to work under the assumption that good literature is often ambiguous, containing subtleties, nuances and varying levels of truth. Characters often represent 'local' and 'global' attributes at different stages of a narrative, or indeed both at once.

iii. Some students forget that they are required to discuss NTG literature as *literature*; the ability to refer to a writer's poetic devices or use of plot, characterisation and setting to convey symbols and metaphors is as necessary to succeed in Extension One as it is to identify the relationship between local cultures and new global forces which exert pressure upon their existence.

iv. Students often approach a dangerously literal position by focusing on the 'local' or 'global' aspects of a given text – ignoring the broader question of the dynamic relationship between the two entities. Similarly, they do not questioning whether the idea of separate 'local' and a 'global' entity is wholly reliable or even a plausible notion.

v. To a certain extent, all students make the initial assumption that the 'local' represents everything noble, wholesome and spiritually fulfilling, while the 'global' is inescapably artificial, opportunistic and morally unconscionable. The threat of clichéd thinking always looms in a class who refuse to do the conceptual 'hard-yards'. Such clichés include the notion that all NTG texts are narratives about the triumphant relocation of the protagonist from a megacity to a local community; a geographical retreat that teaches them the uniqueness of place, the hollow nature of mass-communication and the homogenised values of the twentieth century. Worse still, some students presume the whole course to be a study of the Americanisation of the world.

vi. Extension students need to be open-minded about how they apply the concept of NTG to each prescribed text. They are best to consider the possibility that the concept can be arrived at through a *pluralist* position – a theoretical approach which defines NTG in a way *appropriate to a given text*. As a follow on from this, some related texts may suit one related text more than another. Sometimes there is an assumption that any book referencing the global or local will suit all prescribed texts in the elective. You are advised to select related texts carefully.

The argument for globalisation:

Globalisation has effectively reduced the barriers of time and space. It has increased our awareness of foreign cultures and brought about a common understanding of international political issues affecting minority groups. It has also brought much needed medicine and education to otherwise remote corners of the world. Moreover, the widespread response of the West in response to aid requests from all over the globe demonstrates that the global world has largely promoted empathy and compassion for people once considered remote, exotic and dangerous. A word like *tsunami* demonstrates the global (and democratic) nature of English. No sooner do we attempt to describe a tidal wave than we reach for a Japanese word; for a feeling of studied boredom, *ennui* (French); for an exaggerated illustration, *caricature* (Italian); for political and economic reform, *perestroika* (Russian). This liberal borrowing of the languages of the world underscores the essentially open and democratic nature of our global language – a language that derives its great expressive qualities through tolerance and acceptance of divergent 'local' words. It furthermore underscores the pragmatism and expediency of the emerging global culture.

It is often said by economists that money has no colour, morals or religion. It just is and yet it speaks to everyone. People see it differently but few can live without it, even in the most underdeveloped nations and cultures. Money now moves at the click of a button and has no borders. Some see it as a religion, others as the 'devil incarnate' and it can control all aspects of our lives. The love of it, can be, "the root of all evil." There is more money than ever before in the world. The argument is over its distribution and this is what these texts explore among other issues. Marxist literary theory can be applied to a reading of such texts and links to economic paradigms.

Air travel now draws together any two nations within the span of a single day. Foreigners once considered distant and remote are now regarded as 'near-neighbours' as a result of new technologies which bridge barriers of time and space. Foreign languages and cultures are more accessible and appealing. Furthermore, foreign trade has made our lives more comfortable and intellectually stimulating, while information is more readily accessible. History has taught us that the spread of globalisation is inevitable and might be termed a human 'instinct.' Even the earliest humans migrated and sought to know and borrow from foreign cultures. Travel accounts for the spread of the alphabet, boating technology, instruments of war, and even the spread of oranges, strawberries and the humble potato into Europe.

Globalisation emancipates people from their environment. It has freed many from bondage to the land and from laborious agricultural practices. Globalisation expands our leisure time and 'reduces' space through the advent of airline travel. It democratises knowledge and increases awareness of traditionally exotic cultures; it creates the means for communication, friendship and cooperation between once disparate people; it bonds and unites the developed (first world) to the so-called developing or 'third world'.

Social mobility makes the avenues of political power more accessible. It leads to greater citizen participation in events which affect day-to-day lives. It creates democratic opportunities; grants people market choice and political agency; bestows trade liberalisation in textiles which has led to greater choices in fashion. In short, our new autonomy is underscored by an intellectual freedom to participate in whichever hobby, pursuit or discourse we please. This will not occur, however, when basic needs have not been met.

Globalisation has led to news information becoming immediate and has created a global 'space'. Globalisation has led to the exportation of vital medicines and education to impoverished countries and led to significant advances in accessing information on many topics including health.

Globalisation has led to active citizenship through the internet and television so that world causes are more prominent in the public mind. The advent of information technology allows us to experience global events in an immediate and participatory manner. We furthermore 'vote' in the global economy by endorsing Transnational Corporations and companies who import desirable goods. The trade liberalisation of the world has had an effect on the shape of national labour forces, and obliterates ineffective industries. Modern economies require a flexible, educated workforce. In this way, globalisation is not merely pragmatic or opportunistic, it is a liberator of local economies and their union dominated work forces – it fights against the irrationality of maintaining unproductive work practices.

A world consciousness was created as a result of a popular culture movement in 1984s Live Aid concerts. Bono Vox met George Bush in 2004. As a leader of *popular* culture Bono was powerful in his ability to swing democratic votes and Bush, as a leader of *political* culture, realised the fact. Business leaders such as Bill Gates and Warren Buffett have taken the lead in developing technologies and cures for diseases such as AIDS by using their wealth. Furthermore, global technologies democratise power itself. The famous United Colours of Benetton advertisement in the late 1980s inferred that to be a modern person was to embrace the civilised ideas of multiculturalism – it emotively portrayed images of racial tolerance to demonstrate that globalisation was a liberating force for the world's oppressed nations.

Globalisation creates commodities out of once traditional and isolated communities. Their culture and beliefs are placed onto a wider market place to return a *local* profit for those same communities. Globalisation makes us wealthier, more informed and more aware than ever before.

The video clip and performance of Beyoncé's song "Formation" proved controversial at the 2016 Super Bowl. Research this and explore the issues it raises in light of the module and elective. Perhaps you might like to explore its use as a related text.

More to the point, the western world has no conception of what it means to live in any other sort of way. We are now accustomed to live in a global world and to enjoy its benefits. Personally and environmentally, there is also growing awareness of the costs of globalisation.

The argument against globalisation:

Everything argued (with the exception of the aid and private funded charity) underscores the essentially hollow nature of globalisation and its ultimate benefits for the richest one-quarter (or less) of the world's population. Globalisation is synonymous with expediency, accessibility, capitalism, rampant opportunism, exploitation of labour, shallow values and token knowledge of foreign cultures. The internet provides neither accurate nor 'deep' knowledge – it merely replaces sensory or *empirical* knowledge with the dubious benefit of screen text. Our knowledge of the world is increasingly filtered through the most accessible and unreliable mediums (television and the internet). News reports can lean towards the formulaic, commercial variety and are, at times, unreliable and dubiously loaded with bias.

In as much as starving Africans and displaced refugees are displayed on our television and computer screens and exist only twenty four hours away by aircraft, we increasingly believe that their problems are more easily solved and that others will come to their rescue. International coverage of regional tragedies, coupled with our own expedient natures, makes us believe that such disasters are largely resolved by one-off donations. Viewers can become desensitised.

Worse still, our empathetic reaction to such disasters relies upon the emotive value of their media coverage. In 2008, the human tragedy unfolding in Burma as a result of Typhoon Nagas was quickly superseded in our minds by the horrific images of the earthquake in China a few days later; in 2009 we all gave generously to the Red Cross appeal for Victorians made homeless by bush fires while celebrities appeared on television to question the amount of foreign aid donated by our federal government in response to the Asian tsunami five years earlier. We prioritise our empathy for fellow human beings according to what is presented to us in the most graphic visual terms. The refugee crisis in Europe is a recent concerning global issue and some are demanding a breaking down of territorial boundaries.

In terms of our own lives, the advent of information technology has led to an increase in the demands placed upon us by the corporate world, so that we no longer truly belong to families in the traditional sense, but rather draw on the word *family* in a metaphorical sense, as in "I belong to the corporate family", to which might be added the rejoinder, "with whom I spend most of my time".

Knowledge is increasingly bland, superficial and focused on gossip and entertainment. We have abandoned ethical principles in our dealings with others because all that is important are legal principles – everything is fair game in our expedient and opportunistic new paradigm. Traditional morality and ethics are no longer a common feature in our literary and cinematic narratives because we actively avoid deeper truths in our search for entertainment and in the 'escapism' of computer games and stimulation of new technologies.

Because of our new technologies (i (whatevers), tablets, smartphones and GPS systems) we constantly know *where* we are, but are losing interest in *who* we are. Knowledge meanwhile is universal, but is merely a commodity to be traded for university degrees and commercial transactions. Knowledge for knowledge's sake is no longer valued.

Globalisation promised broader tolerance for foreign cultures but multiculturalism has met with mixed success at the beginning of the 21st century. It was, ironically, stymied by the spread of liberal democratic traditions (a concept itself ushered in to facilitate the spread of capitalism). Populist sentiment is allowed to prevail under the western parliamentary model and consequently immigration has become a contentious political issue in Western countries over the last few decades and the last few years in particular. Consider how divisive the 'Boat People' issue is in Australia and the extreme opinions over the refugee crisis around the globe. On September 7th, 2015, the BBC reported,

> *Chancellor Angela Merkel has said the "breathtaking" flow of migrants into Germany will "occupy and change" the country in the coming years.*

Has our compassion for political and economic refugees increased with the advent of information technology which presents visual images to make us aware of their plight? A photo of a small drowned boy in the arms of a soldier swept the globe in 2016 and engendered much sympathy. While constant bombardment can desensitise, the occasional image can spark a united effort.

New beliefs in universal knowledge, have led to scepticism and abandonment of inductive and empirical reasoning. In turn, 'rational' enquiry (the reliance on science to answer metaphysical questions we once sought through philosophical enquiry – questions fundamental to our sense of ontology and epistemology), has become popular. Thus, it may be argued that scientific arguments are replacing the philosophical in a globalised world.

Consider too that the increase in global pharmaceuticals will lead to an increase in the world's population, thus having an ultimately destructive consequence upon the world's resources.

Globalisation furthermore, presents a *hypnopaedia* of sorts. It trivialises totemic cultural items and commodifies. It creates divisions between rich and poor – leading to the exploitation of foreign labour.

The more we embrace globalisation, the more we destroy the planet. Globalisation is a new form of empire. While the Romans exported power through military authority and others have exercised power through religious control, the new empire of globalisation largely spreads its power through images and money. Corporations and technology are new powers. As just another opportunistic worldwide movement, historically it may be equally destined to fail – as the global, economic meltdown (GFC) in 2009 perhaps already demonstrated.

The value of free association towards creating an original definition

It may also be useful to have students frame their own definitions of NTG by free association with the term.

Such an exercise may begin with a consideration about the different forms of the verb *to navigate*.

The word 'navigate' originates from the Latin *navigatus*; *navis* translating as 'ship' and *igare* translating as 'drive'. Thus, the title of the course refers to the way that individuals and societies drive, steer and hence manage lives in a global world.

Each of the texts set for study explores ways in which individuals manage their lives in a global world. Some manage to navigate successfully whilst others are challenged or simply shy away from the task. In each instance it can lead to positive and negative outcomes for the individual.

Students should explore a range of statements and problems associated with NTG. Alternatively, teachers might simply pick apart ideas for the purpose of generating classroom debate about the theoretical implications of the concept.

Statements

- The individual who navigates the global retreats from mass communication: the internet, mobile phone and television news coverage. They commence a personal exploration.

- The individual who navigates the global becomes distant from the attitude of *conqueror knows best* and the historical bias of victorious nations. They, furthermore, distance themselves from the lies of 'race' and nationalism.

- The individual who navigates a global perspective of the world denies the notion of a 'correct' reading of ancient superstitions, religious practices, traditional customs and beliefs.

- The individual who navigates the global is wary of the lingua franca of English and instead embraces local dialects.

- The individual who navigates the global denies the fiction of global order (UN); the global village (television); the lies of 'global' militaries (USA); and the ethical right of a free-market economy to create an *underclass* or 'third world' of human beings. They question the superficiality of 'global' knowledge which supposes to tell the grand truths of human history. Marxism; psychoanalysis; science; economic theory and religion are given due consideration when Navigating the Global. Ways of thinking lie at the heart of values formation and help to steer directions and outcomes in a navigation of the global. This is seen in themes, characterisation and p[lot development in texts.

Problems

- What is the slippery nature of theorising a global world? How do you navigate *away* from the 'global' once you have embraced its supposed benefits?

- Who can ever be said to stand outside the social and intellectual trends of their times?

- What is the nature of a specifically 'local' context as opposed to a 'global' context?

- What is the meaningful division between 'local' and 'global' knowledge?

- Who may claim to represent local culture? Who can legitimately claim in turn not to have been affected by global culture?

Summary

Are we ever able to firmly align ourselves with either a local or a global community? Can we logically divorce ourselves from the influence of either world? Will globalisation succeed and thrive or ultimately collapse? Is it the determining model for the future as economic and political borders continue to be challenged? 'Navigating the Global' is best understood as a fluid concept; a theoretical prism, well-defined, yet nevertheless adaptable to the distinctive cultural milieu of each composer.

THE COMPOSER

Denise Levertov, Poet

Denise Levertov (1923–1997) was born in Essex, England. She was home schooled and grew up surrounded with culture and learning. Her father was a muilti-lingual Russian Jew who converted to Christianity and became an Anglican minister. Levertov met and married American writer Mitchell Goodman and moved to the United States. In 1955, she became an American citizen.

She published at least fifteen volumes of poetry, including *Selected Poems* (Newcastle upon Tyne, 1986) and *Breathing the Water* (New York, 1987; Newcastle upon Tyne, 1988). Prose works include *The Poet in the World* (New York 1973) and *Light Up the Cave* (New York, 1981). Levertov taught at many universities and was a professor of English at Stanford University.

Levertov showed an enthusiasm for writing from an early age. She was 17 when she published her first poem and she exhibited ambition in sending some of her poems to T.S.Eliot. Levertov served in London as a civilian nurse in the Blitz, during WWII, so had first hand experience of the devastating effects of war. Her first volume of poems, *The Double Image*, was published in 1946. Political themes emerged in poetry written in the 1960s and 70s. Levertov's poetry became more political at this time and she became aligned with feminist and leftist activist poets.

After Levertov moved to the United States, the Black Mountain Poets, known as avant-garde post modern poets, influenced her way of thinking and writing. Levertov was especially affected by Charles Olson, an American Modernist poet. The experimental style of poets like Olson and Ezra Pound took shape in her own poetry, manifesting itself in her emerging ideas and break from a more traditional poetic form. Further influenced by transcendentalism, which encompassed complex philosophical and religious ideas, Levertov was able to channel these philosophies and ways of thinking which often questioned human's existence and purpose, into her own writing. Levertov's conversion to Christianity in 1984 greatly influenced her later work although religious themes characterised much of her poetry. Her later poems were assured in their tone whereas earlier poems offered the hope of the Christian message in a questioning rather than assured way. Levertov became certain that hostile social environments could be changed by individuals with Christian values. (Dewey, Anne. "The Art of the Octopus: The Maturation of Denise Levertov's Political Vision." Renascence(sic) 50 (1998): 65–81.)

Her attitude to socio- political themes might be described in the oxymoron, militant pacifism. She saw people united through a common spiritual heritage and sharing responsibility for a shared planet.

The Vietnam War was pivotal in reshaping and developing Levertov's poetry. She openly resisted the war by joining the War Resister's League, a nonviolent revolutionary group. Much of her political poetry deals with the consequences of war, loss and the destruction of culture and history. As a writer, Levertov believed it was important, a duty even, to highlight the injustice of conflict and war. There is a very real call for change in her poems within this period, as the emerging homogenisation of mass culture operating within a paradigm of violence, forces poets like her to make their voices heard. Levertov promotes the idea that individuals have a duty to challenge the establishment and become advocates of change, no matter how small, often developing a personal questioning voice, which can often be confronting for the reader.

Themes in her poetry include suffering, terror, loss, violence and apathy. However, there are flashes of hope embedded within the poems. There is often a juxtaposition of beauty and horror in her poems in an attempt to remind the reader of the complexities of humanity. Levertov shows how suffering has become mundane, an everyday occurrence, which stifles any ability to communicate effectively and extinguishes individuality or creativity. This stripping of humanity presents a challenge for the reader as, at times, the graphic imagery provokes a striking reality of war that is inescapable. Levertov continued writing and giving readings, despite her declining health. She died of complications due to lymphoma on December 20, 1997.

Quotes from https://www.poetryfoundation.org/poems-and-poets/poets/detail/denise-levertov cast further light on this poet. Amy Gerstler in the Los Angeles Times Book Review claimed that, a "reader poking her nose into any Levertov book at random finds herself in the presence of a clear uncluttered voice — a voice committed to acute observation and engagement with the earthly, in all its attendant beauty, mystery and pain." Contemporary themes such as, Eros, solitude, community, war emerge in Levertoff's poetry yet her approach to the concerns of her time was, as Rexroth claimed, "...classically independent."

CONTEXT

Levertov's Poetic Context

The decades stemming from the 1960s to the 1980s saw social and protest movements for civil rights, peace and feminism. These were followed in the early 1970s by the environmental movement and anti-nuclear demonstrations. In the United States many traditional systems of thought were being challenged – political, racial, social, and religious. Levertov found herself playing the role of the political activist through her poetry.

The Vietnam War, 1955-75

During the 1960s, Levertov's poetry was increasingly linked to and inspired by the political turmoil and events of the times and also to Levertov's personal involvement as an activist in various protest movements. Levertov wrote her first overtly political poetry during the Vietnam War. Levertov not only called for an end to the Vietnam War but also for action against the systems of oppression at home in order to solve the problems those systems created— problems of sexism, racism, pollution, and social injustice.

1970s and 1980s – Environmental degradation and the threat of nuclear warfare.

For Levertov the 70s and 80s were unprecedented times. Unlike the Vietnam War of the 1960s, the amassing of nuclear weapons had catastrophic global implications which endangered humanity's very existence. Levertov displays anxiety over the destruction of the natural world in her poetry. She also expresses her fear of nuclear warfare and humanity's destruction.

1980s – Reconciling differences

Whilst Levertov spent decades opposing war, in the late 1980s she proposed an alternative, making peace. The late 1980s were for Levertov a time of reconciling differences. She felt that in order to solve the problems that her contemporary society was faced with; problems of human relationships as well as environmental degradation, people needed to realise how humans were part of the fabric of nature, interconnected in a multitude of ways to the rest of creation. As a result, her poetry became more spiritual and religious and included an abundance of Christian imagery. Levertov felt that her poetry had a significant social function; to open the reader to greater compassion and empathy through the most essential element of human capacity –the imagination.

THE POEMS

'What Were They Like?' (1966)

In this poem Levertov explores the impact of globalisation and homogenisation of cultures. It is set in a nightmarish dystopian future in which cultural memory and history have been erased by war. It explores the way American warfare and military action during the Vietnam War will have impacted Vietnamese history, culture and values. Levertov warns the readers of globalisation's threat to the extinction of a culture's traditions, values, language and paradigms.

'The Sun Going Down upon Our Wrath' (1972)

Levertov worries about the young and their innocence regarding mankind's corrupt and destructive ways. She does not want to paint too bleak a picture as it may prove futile and not inspire change in ways of thinking in the young. She hopes that there is still time to reverse the damage that has been created by mankind so far.

'The Malice of Innocence' (1972)

Levertov reflects on her role as a civilian nurse in England in World War 2. She reflects on the institutional paradigms of the hospital which guided her ways of thinking. She was ambitious and wanted to succeed. She prided herself on being meticulous, ordered, and on completing her duties successfully. However, this came at a cost. She realised many years later that in the process of achieving her goals she forgot to exercise her humanity and compassion as a nurse.

'A Place of Kindness' (1975)

In this poem Levertov longs for a place free from corruptive forces. She longs for a place that is free from globalisation's homogenisation, economic paradigms, cunning, violence and associated atrocities.

'What it Could Be' (1975)

Levertov explores the impact of environmental destruction as a result of uranium mining as well as humanity's annihilation through nuclear warfare. She often protested nuclear testing, carrying placards at demonstrations saying 'stop the testing'. Levertov acknowledged her fear for the escalating nuclear arms race between the USA and the Soviet Union by saying that 'the worst thing is nuclear threat.' She demonstrated against the construction of the Seabrook nuclear power plant.

'Life of Others' (1978)

In this poem Levertov acknowledges that the only way humanity can navigate the global successfully is to unite and to revert to religious and philosophical ways of thinking. She offers a bleak image of humanity floundering in a blind haze of corruption where the individual does not have the capability to navigate successfully if they choose to do so on their own.

'Talk in the Dark' (1982)

Levertov's poem exposes the terror faced by individuals in an increasingly globalised world that greets violence with violence. She explores the loss of humanity in the wake of nuclear warfare and references the atomic bombing of Hiroshima in Japan by the United States during the final stages of World War 2. The atomic bombings of Hiroshima and Nagasaki at the end of World War 2 remain the first and only use of nuclear weapons in warfare. Both bombings caused the death of approximately 250 000 people.

SUMMARISING YOUR POETRY NOTES

How to construct poem summary sheets

Whilst your teacher may take you through each of the poems set for study, or while you may analyse the poems in groups in class or on your own, it is important that you write up your own summary sheets in order to consolidate the information that you have written down, heard or discussed in class. The following grid provides you with a list of areas to help you construct your poetry summary sheets. You could devise your own poetry sheets and even extend those provided here. Consider adding space to comment on themes and the message.

Title	What does the title mean? What is the effect of the title?
Audience	Who is the intended audience?
Purpose	Why was this poem written? (e.g. persuade, inform, entertain?)
Context	What is the context behind the creation of this poem?
Key concepts	What are the key ideas the poet is exploring?
Tone	What is the composer's attitude?
Structure	Comment on the structure of the poem. Does it reflect any of the key ideas in the poem? Look at overall structure as well as stanza structure and sentence structure. Is the structure traditional or modern?
Word choice and language devices	Are there any examples of: alliteration, anaphora, antithesis, assonance, allusions, analogy, apostrophe, asyndeton, connotations, hyperbole, imperative, irony, jargon, metaphor, motif, onomatopoeia, oxymoron, paradox, personification, polysyndeton, pun, repetition, sibilance, simile, symbols, synecdoche, rhetorical questions?
Punctuation	Is there any unusual punctuation used? What is the effect of the punctuation? Are there examples of enjambment, endstopping, ellipsis or caesuras?
Rhythm and metre	Is the metre regular or irregular? Is the metre iambic? Does the poem use trimetre, tetrametre, pentametre? Is it free verse? What is the effect of these choices?

Here is an empty grid for you to fill out as a summary sheet for each of your poems. Consider printing it on A3 paper and completing one on each poem, for your revision.

	Response	Support for Response-Textual Reference
What is the Title?		
Who is the audience?		
What is the purpose of this poem?		
What is the context of this poem?		
What is the context within this poem?		

© Five Senses Education Pty Ltd

What are the Ways of Thinking in this poem?		
What is the overall tone?		
Identify the message and themes		
What kind of poetic structure is used?		
What is the significance behind the word choice and language devices Levertov uses?		
Is there anything unusual about the punctuation?		

How is the rhythm and metre used?		
How does Levertov explore Navigating the Global in this poem?		

Additional points and comments:

ANALYSIS OF POEMS

'What Were They Like?' From *Poems 1960–67 ©1966*

Synopsis

The poem is presented in two parts and examines the devastation of a local culture, customs and way of life lost due to conflict. The way of life is presented as precious, simple and ancient. The poem begins with a series of questions contemplating what the Vietnamese people were once like. The narrator appears to be ignorant about the culture and customs of a people.

In the second part of the poem, the questions are answered and the poet includes parallel imagery of stone lanterns, flowers, bones, laughter, children and poetry. However, the narrator's investigation into an ancient culture ends with a depressing silence as there are no longer any people with whom to share or pass on the culture. ..."after the children were killed/There were no more buds."..."It is silent now."

The investigative tone is reinforced with use of formal language and the repetition of the opening word, "Did" throughout the first stanza. This is in contrast with the rest of the poem which uses informal language.

A thematic concern in the poem is memory. Levertov emphasises the importance of memory in passing on stories and culture. Her lament of Vietnam's violent past is prevalent in the unemotional tone of the first part and the definitive, resigned tone at the poem's close. Levertov represents global conflict as having utterly destroyed old ways of thinking and living. The simplistic, idyllic way of life irrevocably changed and in the place of a once-thriving, rich culture, came emptiness and silence.

Significant quotes

- 'Did the people of Vietnam/use lanterns of stone?'
- '...after the children were killed/there were no more buds'
- 'It is not remembered. Remember/most were peasants'
- 'Maybe fathers told their sons old tales'
- 'There is an echo yet /of their speech which was like a song'
- 'Who can say? It is silent now.'

Techniques and references

Levertov's simple, direct questions in the first part of the poem, listed 1–6 are in past tense to highlight that the people and their culture is lost. In the title, the narrator questions 'What Were They Like?', presenting a universal ignorance of a lost past. The cause of this loss of communication, in the form of oral tradition and telling stories, is due to global conflict. The repeated phrase, 'it is not remembered,' highlights the obliteration of collective memory. The past tense and definitive, high modality tone emphasises loss of local culture which has been destroyed by violence.

The narrator imagines the Vietnamese people as a primitive yet peaceful and reserved race. The imagery of worship through light and ceremony is revealed with the locals being described as using 'lanterns of stone' and 'hold[ing] ceremonies to reverence the opening of buds.' The ritual of welcoming new life is presented through the positive imagery of 'opening buds', implying a simple joy in the cycle of nature. However, this harmony and peace is contrasted later in the poem with parallel imagery as the people's 'light hearts are turned to stone.' There is no celebration and a sense of immobilisation and emotional hardness take precedence in the metaphor. People's hearts have become stone-like, after having been tainted by war and conflict. The buds can no longer open, as 'after the children were killed/there were no more buds.' The totality of the destruction is more profound as nature and children are both innocent. Levertov implies that globalisation, in this case symbolised as war, has violently destroyed everything in its path. The death of the land and the people heralds a death of innocence.

A localised, reserved and simple way of life is established in the poem. Levertov presents the local people as being 'inclined to quiet laughter'. Their language seems musical. The narrator questions, 'Did they distinguish between speech and singing?' Voices are symbolic of communication and this motif of voices is explored in the poem. However, the local voices are quiet and delicate. Levertov implies that the local is fragile and easily disrupted or fragmented. Although their speech is seemingly positive, described as 'laughter,' their voices become lost by the end of the poem, resulting in silence. The positive connotations of laughter are contrasted in the negative imagery of 'laughter is bitter to the burned mouth' where the alliterative, contextual reference to Napalm, reminds the reader that the destruction is savage.

Furthermore, the plosive alliteration in 'bitter' and 'burned' highlights Levertov's own agenda in the poem, her condemnation of the Vietnam war and its consequences. At the height of this condemnation, the narrator imagines that when the 'bombs smashed' there was 'time only to scream'. This provides auditory juxtaposition from the earlier, quieter laughter. Voices diminish throughout the poem and are eventually referred to as an 'echo... which was like a song...' which 'resembled the flight of moths in moonlight.' The alliteration of 'moths in moonlight' coupled with metaphor, further epitomise the fragility of the local and the resultant destruction of the collective, human spirit.

Levertov implies that the oral tradition of telling stories is fundamental to maintaining culture. She grants a flicker of hope as a better, simpler life is revealed, through the poet's description of a more pastoral, bucolic lifestyle prior to the advent of globalisation. The narrator commands responders to 'Remember/ most were peasants; their life /was in rice and bamboo.' The enjambment and caesurae create pauses in the text, allowing the narrator to speak, in a seemingly natural manner, directly to the reader. Syntax and a tone of high modality forces responders to focus on the foregrounded word 'remember' which highlights the importance of memory. The rice and bamboo become metonyms of the agrarian Vietnamese way of life, which is valued. The need for stories and myths is further valued as the narrator imagines a life 'when peaceful clouds were reflected in the paddies...maybe fathers told their sons old tales.' The peaceful, visual imagery and reflection provides a perfect setting for the passing down of traditions. Shared culture from father to son, enables traditions to be valued and preserved.

It is clear that by the end of the poem, a damaging global influence has wrought disruption and destroyed the local beyond repair. The tone of resigned defeat is overwhelming in the final line, 'Who can say? It is silent now.' The monosyllabic question emphasises the lack of knowledge and inability to find out about ancient cultures, as there is no one left to ask. We are left with ambiguity as the lack of an ability to communicate with one another is due to the fact that in a quest to gain through one paradigm, much has been destroyed in another. Without communication and a passing down of values, attitudes and traditions, cultures end. The despondent tone is, therefore, bleak both in itself and for what it represents.

Links to Ways of Thinking

Levertov uses this poem as a stark reminder that in our increasingly globalised world, we no longer have the ability to connect; we have become so alienated from one another through a discourse of destruction that there will be no one left – we will exterminate ourselves. The localised way of thinking is presented as preferable but not realistic. The poet realises the importance of language as a preserver of identity and culture. Although this is not explicit, she warns the reader that humanity is fragile and in our attempt to control, we will simultaneously wield power, fall prey to it and kill what we once valued. This is an indictment of the postmodern condition, as boundaries and concepts become increasingly blurred and result in a fragmentation of self. Once this occurs, we become alienated and meaning is harder to grasp. In this ever-shifting reality, it perhaps becomes easier to destroy one another due to an increasing state of human indifference. Also, with the advent of technological warfare, which Levertov condemns, the individual is granted a certain amount of distance from their actions. The echoes of the past in her poetry serve as a caution, a plea, not to forget our humanity.

Questions

1. Why does the poem open with a series of questions?

2. Why is the word "perhaps" used in the reply?

3. What connotations does the word "buds" have and what is the significance of there being," no more buds"?

4. Referencing the contents of this poem, outline some of the ways the people of Vietnam were impacted by the war.

5. Find an example of sibilance being used to convey a peaceful image and a violent image. What other techniques are seen in your examples and what is their effect?

6. Research: lanterns of stone.

7. This is poem about memory, tradition and culture and it is overlaid with loss.

   Justify this statement   with close reference to the poem.

8. How do you see Levertov exploring issues which are linked to the concept of Navigating the Global, within this poem?

'Sun Going Down upon Our Wrath' From *Poems 1968-72* ©*1972*

Synopsis

The poem deals with Levertov's concerns about how writers or poets, can warn future generations about mankind's destructive ways. There is a sense of danger in repeating the past. Yet, if the warning is too harsh, it may prove futile and not inspire any change in future ways of thinking. Levertov is cautious. With knowledge, comes responsibility and shedding of one's innocence, or in this case, beauty. The veneer of 'childish faces' which are seemingly beautiful, may be 'scale[d] off' to reveal ugliness and decay. The knowledge which is gained will tarnish not enlighten. With this image of revelation comes misery and the destruction of innocence, highlighting the atrocities mankind is capable of and the sacrifice one must make with acquiring new knowledge of the world's misery and pain.

Levertov reminds responders of the writer's duty to teach and impress upon future generations, the mistakes of the past. Here, the context is firmly referring to the atrocities of the Vietnam War, its carnage and destruction of a culture and way of life. Levertov uses mythological and religious references to ancient civilisations or individuals of power, to reveal the importance of learning from history or epic mythological stories. The questions posed in the poem confront the reader. Responders are presented with Levertov's views of rejecting violence.

Significant quotes

- 'Do you already know/what hope is fading from us/ and pay no heed?'

- 'Is there an odyssey/ your feet pull you towards/ away from now to walk/ the waters...?'

- 'It seems your fears are only the old fears, antique/ anxieties, how graceful;'

- 'If you are warned will your beauty/ scale off, to leave/ gaping meat livid with revulsion?'

- 'If there is time to warn you...if you were warned and believed the warning'

- ' a wall of refusal'

- 'could there be/ a reversal I cannot hoist myself enough/ to see,/ plunge myself deep enough/ to know?

Techniques and references

The poem's title includes an inter textual Biblical reference to Ephesians 4:26. It is quoted here from the King James version, 'Be ye angry, and sin not: let not the sun go down on your wrath.' This sets the tone for the rest of the poem. The warning is ambiguous in part. It can mean anger is sin and further sin will result, if there is no forgiveness. We are urged to end anger before nightfall and reconcile differences. The inclusive pronoun 'our' in the title suggests readers are implicated in the 'wrath' or hatred. Clearly, the message of the poem mirrors this biblical teaching, but Levertov also implies that it is almost too late. The sun is already setting on humanity's wrath, cursing them to live in sin and hate for eternity unless they act. The statement of the title presents the lack of forgiveness as a surety rather than an option. The visual imagery of the sun setting connotes hope fading. Traditionally, light and dark symbolise good and evil. Therefore, the fading light of day implies the hope being lost for any chance of absolution.

The speaker of the poem uses direct second person address in the opening sentence, 'You who are so beautiful–' addressing the audience, stating that, in their youth, they are beautiful. The elliptical dash at the end of the line creates a wistful pause implying that this beauty is fragile and naïve. Their innocence is furthered with the adjectival reference to the people being 'childish'. The question following this stanza stands alone, 'shall I warn you?' emphasising that the speaker knows more than the audience and has the power to take away their innocence with knowledge of the truth. The choice to warn or not, lies with the speaker, or writer, reinforcing Levertov's belief that it is her duty to write didactically, to tell the truth as she perceives it. The imperative tone is a reminder that ignorance is preferred: that the truth can corrupt or destroy.

Levertov continues the poem with a series of questions challenging responders' ways of thinking about the changes wrought by war. She asks, 'Do you know/ what it was to have/ a certitude of grasses waving/ upon the earth…' The predictability of nature's cycles, is no longer certain to some cultures or people due to war, which is furthered by the past tense 'was'. The positive visual imagery of grass personified, 'waving', seems friendly and welcoming. However, this image is juxtaposed starkly with the conjunction that follows '…**though** all humankind were dust?' proving that despite the innocence of some, many others were suffering. The dust is a contextual reference to the Vietnam war that decimated thousands and reduced a whole culture. Further, the dust also alludes the book of Genesis *3:19*, '…for dust thou art, and unto dust shalt thou return.' Although, Levertov's account of their return to the earth as dust is ironic in the phrase, 'Of dust returning/ to **fruitful** dust?' The emphasis on 'fruitful' is evidence of her bitterness that their deaths are *not* fruitful, but actually wasteful. Another interpretation may highlight mankind in human form being less fruitful than in the form of dust, especially when man wages war and displays anger towards fellow humans.

Further, Levertov questions the existence of hope in a world of such chaos and asks of her audience, 'Do you already know/ what hope is fading from us...?' The negative diction and imagery of 'fading' is reminiscent of the sun setting, as mentioned in the title. The hope for different ways of thinking to save future human existence is disappearing and the tone becomes more accusatory. Also, the inclusive pronoun 'us' implies all are involved in the process, not just a few, which is indicative of a more globalised way of thinking, where individualism is promoted over adopting a collective mentality. This is clearly revealed in the phrase 'and pay no heed' where Levertov accuses the audience of ignoring others' plights.

The poem refers to the journey of the individual as an 'odyssey' which provides a mythological reference to an epic journey of adventure, suggesting that to navigate, one must overcome a range of barriers or influences. However, the speaker implies that this odyssey is drawing them *away* from the present global problems, 'to walk the waters.' Here, the biblical allusion and miracle of Jesus walking on water is clear. The reference to fallen orchard stars is to apples as each apple, when cut across, reveals stars. The fact that the apples have fallen also links back to the fall of man and our human condition. This is related in the book of Genesis in the Bible when Adam and Eve eat of the tree of good and evil after Eve is tempted by the snake. This interpretation is validated through the two rhetorical questions. The first question is, "Shall I warn you?" The second question is, " Can you be warned?". This raises the notion of original sin and the idea that old patterns will be repeated. Perhaps it will need a miracle to avoid man's wrath towards his fellow man.

The speaker continues to warn the audience that once knowledge is gained, innocence and beauty will fade. She begins with the subjunctive 'if' in the phrase, 'if you are warned will your beauty/ scale off, to leave/gaping meat livid with revulsion?' This highlights that choice rests with the audience, to change their way of thinking and choose to learn about the truth. The cost of learning this truth, however, is revealed as Levertov suggests that such truth will strip the knower of their beauty or innocence, to reveal 'gaping meat livid with revulsion' beneath. The graphic imagery heightens her own disgust at people's ignorance, or choices and she reduces such humans to 'meat', items or commodities to be slain by global warfare.

The next two stanzas raise more Biblical allusions and hope is reinforced through the imagery. Even for the speaker who is hard hearted," in whose heart stones rattle", routines exist. They can work and, above all, imagine.

The next stanza opens with a Biblical allusion to Proverbs 4:7 King James Version (KJV), "Wisdom is the principal thing; therefore get wisdom: and with all thy getting get understanding." This hope is seemingly undercut with another reference to the human condition and the reminder that there is nothing new under the sun. (Ecclesiastes 1:9) The "ancient" referred to is King Solomon. He had wisdom yet ultimately, "His future/ rolled away in great coils forever/ into the generations." This would seems to highlight the human condition and that we all return to dust, regardless of our wisdom. Solomon's lineage, however, extended to Christ who offers the ultimate hope and salvation. The second half of the stanza states, "Among conies the grass/

grew again/ and among bones./And the bones would rise." This refers to the book of Ezekiel in the Bible, Chapter 37, verses 1–10. God breathed on the dry bones, breath came to them and they stood up. There is hope rather than hopelessness in this image. It is God who can conquer death and the human condition. The word " conies" is also unfamiliar but refers to a rabbit like animal in the Bible. It is sometimes known as a rock badger.

Levertov continues with the idea that there is a choice and again, suggests that there may be hope yet to come. This is revealed with the subjunctive prefacing the following warning, '**If** there is time to warn you...**if** you were warned and believed the warning...' The poet implies that people do not heed warnings, as a tone of doubt is prevalent in the phrase, further seen in the repetition of 'if'. She questions the integrity of the listener but also the reference to time presents a sense of urgency, as time seems to be running out to change people's way of thinking. Further to this idea that people are stubborn, is the visual imagery and metaphor of 'a wall of refusal'. Levertov is concerned that despite her warnings, people will disbelieve, ignore or refuse to take heed. Since the fall of man, selfishness is part of our collective nature. Will people cling to hopelessness rather than hope, believing the grass will never regrow and the conies became extinct? Would innocence disappear? If the warnings were headed, would innocence transform into "spears of fire...fire to turn fire." This suggests that knowledge may lead to more knowledge as it is transferred, and ultimate change.

The poem ends with a final question 'could there be/ a reversal I cannot hoist myself enough/ to see,/ plunge myself deep enough/ to know?' Here, the speaker questions her own ability to see the truth and challenges her own ways of thinking. She is not outside the context of humanity and cannot perceive objectively. Knowledge is revealed to be a deep well or pool of truth into which she must plunge. It is a difficull decision as the laboured verbs 'hoist' and 'plunge' connote the challenge of this task. Her final question leads to uncertainty which is furthered with the conditional tense 'could'. A spiritual turning to truth and knowledge, wisdom and understanding may bring a political turning away from wrath and anger but the writer cannot ultimately escape her context. The poem was written in 1972. The Vietnam War did not end until April 30th, 1975.

The structure of the poem in irregular line lengths and stanzas, enjambment and caesura, creates a sense of internal chaos and uncertainty about the future. This is furthered by the lack of rhyme as the comfort that comes with uniformity or patterns is no longer available to the speaker or the audience.

Links to ways of thinking

Levertov uses poetry to present a dichotomy between knowledge and ignorance, using different images to examine the fear of and power of knowledge and the apparent beauty of ignorance. The continued emphasis on warning promotes Levertov's aim in changing existing ways of thinking. She hopes responders will adopt a more truthful and aware mind-set. The wealth of Biblical allusions points to man's ways of thinking being changed by God's intervention and an acknowledgement of his omnipotence. Chaos, anger and war aligns with the post modern condition and the age old human condition since the fall of man and the entry of sin into the world. Death is part of the human condition but the hope of the Christian message can free us from death and offer hope when there seems to be none. The collapse of metanarratives can alienate the individual or disperse a collective way of thinking. The acceptance of them and the spread of them can cause revival and transformation. Levertov is known for the inclusion of Christian themes in her poetry. This poem exemplifies the raising and questioning of Christian themes which permeates her poetry before her conversion in 1984. After this date, the questioning gives way to assurances and a tone of higher modality.

Questions

1. Who is the 'you' being addressed in Stanza One?

2. What view of nature is presented in Stanza Two? Support your response with reference to the poem.

3. How is the concept of desensitisation introduced in the poem?

4. What intertextual link is there between the word, "odyssey" and seemingly impossible tasks?

5. Research "orchard stars". How might they be linked to apples? How does the adjective " fallen" operate on several levels to introduce ambiguity and connotation?

6. Comment on the effect of the metaphor, alliteration, temporal references and rhetorical question found towards the end of the poem.

7. How do you see Levertov exploring issues which are linked to the concept of Navigating the Global, within this poem?

'The Malice of Innocence', From *Poems 1968-1972* ©1972

Synopsis

In this poem Levertov sits watching a movie on television. The movie is *Sunday Bloody Sunday*, and a scene from the movie set in a hospital ward, transports her back to a time when she was a nurse in World War Two and worked in several civilian hospitals. Levertov recalls her time in the wards, her experience, her motivations, her insensitivity and evaluates this period of time from her present day perspective. She realises that whilst working in the hospital system she abandoned her conscience, compassion and understanding for a sense of achievement and success. Upon reflection, Levertov realises that her youthful innocence and quest to personally succeed led her to being malicious instead of compassionate towards her patients.

Significant Quotes

- 'A glimpsed world, halfway through the film,/one slow shot of a ward at night'

- 'in the dim long room, warm, orderly,/and full of breathings as a cowbarn.'

- 'listened/ to the wall-clock's pulse, and turn by turn/ the two of us made our rounds/ on tiptoe, bed to bed,'

- 'we were gravely dancing–starched/in our caps, our trained replies,

- our whispering aprons–the well-rehearsed/ pavanne of power.'

- 'Yes, wasn't it power, /and not compassion,/gave our young hearts their hard fervor? '

- 'But I loved the power/ of our ordered nights,/gleaming surfaces I'd helped to polish'

- 'But I got lost in the death rooms a while,/remembering being (crudely, cruelly,/just as a soldier or one of the guards/ from Dachau might be) in love with order,'

- 'an angel like the *chercheuses de poux*, floating /noiseless from bed to bed,'

- 'smoothing pillows, tipping/water to parched lips, writing/ details of agony carefully into the Night Report.'

Techniques and references

The title 'The Malice of Innocence' is, in fact, a paradox. Innocence is associated with goodness while malice is associated with its opposite -evil, so even before the poem begins, Levertov indicates to the reader that there will be a conflict of good and evil unfolding. This conflict will occur as a result of her reflecting on her past actions and motivations from her current adult perspective.

Levertov adopts a meditative pace through her use of form which is generally a two line stanza varied to one or three lines. As a result of this form, the pace is slow. A solemn tone and atmosphere is also created. This solemnity stemmed from Levertov's tense realisation and discovery, as an adult, that she sacrificed compassion and empathy for success, order and discipline when she was a young nurse.

Levertov is inspired to take a trip back in time whilst watching a film on television. The film was *Sunday Bloody Sunday* – a 1971 British Drama directed by John Schlesinger. The film features a 'slow shot of a ward a night' which acts as a catalyst for Levertov to reflect on a time long past when she was a young nurse during World War Two and working in a hospital. The sibilant 's' sound coupled with the low vowel 'ow' lengthen and slow the pace of the opening, showing how Levertov's attention has been captured and that time has indeed slowed down for her at this moment of reflection.

It is significant that she uses the setting of a hospital as this can be seen as a place of both birth and death, hope and despair. It also reminds the audience of the paradox in the title and of how good and evil can coexist. In Levertov's reflection, the hospital represents death, pain and weakness and therefore acts as a metaphorical criticism of humanity's sickness and decaying morals that come as a result of wholeheartedly embracing institutional paradigms. Thus, the poem can be seen as an extended metaphor of humanity's failings and inherent 'sickness' in adopting the global institutions' ways of thinking. It is also interesting to note that historically hospitals were founded by religious orders or charitable individuals and leaders, as opposed to today's government bodies and private owners. The word hospital is also closely linked to the word 'hospitality' which means to be friendly towards guests; however, the word became far removed from this meaning in Levertov's cold and routine world.

When Levertov's flashback takes her back into a hospital ward, her immediate association is not with people, but rather tangible objects such as a 'Greenshaded lamp glowing/on the charge desk/

clipboards stacked on the desk for the night.' The listing here gives a sense of order and the crisp 't' sounds add to the sense of organisation. She begins to recall the patients; however, the language is depersonalised and detached in tone. Levertov waits for 'morning stirrings' in a room that is 'warm, orderly and full of breathings as a cowbarn.' Again, listing is used and this time it is coupled with a simile that further detaches Levertov from the patient's humanity.

Levertov recalls her time as a nurse on a hospital ward as being one of 'rhythm, a choreographic decorum:' Here Levertov utilises music and dance jargon to show how her nightly visits to the patients were a choreographed routine and that there was a sense of show and performance on her part to complete her rounds. Once again, this detached her from their humanity. There is a continued use of dance jargon when Levertov remembers how , in this autobiographical poem, 'we were gravely dancing–starched/ in our caps, our trained replies,/our whispering aprons–the well-rehearsed/ pavanne of power.' A pavanne is a slow dance and here Levertov links it to her feelings of power and control over the patients. She remembers the motivation behind her 'performance' of duties – power rather than compassion. Her use of rhetorical question 'Yes, wasn't it power, /and not compassion,/gave our young hearts/their hard fervor?' shows her growing awareness that she was indeed lacking compassion towards the patients and instead, wanting to feel success and achievement for herself. 'But I loved the power/ of our ordered nights,/gleaming surfaces I'd helped to polish'. Here the adjective 'gleaming' suggests something clean, cold and clinical and further reinforces that she was more connected to satisfying the objectives of her work than to helping the patients.

Levertov's complete understanding of her motivations as a young nurse occurs when she compares herself in a simile to 'a soldier or one of the guards/from Dachau'. She realises that her motives were selfish and she showed a lack of empathy and detachment from what she did. The historical reference to the Dachau concentration camp is particularly chilling and reinforces Levertov's extreme criticism of her insensitive behaviour and cold attitude as a young nurse.

Levertov ends the poem with an image of her ' smoothing pillows, tipping water to parched lips, writing details of agony carefully in the Night Report.' Here the listing provides a contrast between her being a compassionate nurse and a clinical executor of a task. 'Smoothing pillows' and 'tipping water into parched lips' are soothing and comforting images however, 'writing details' of agony is insensitive, cold and clinical in comparison. The use of the adjective 'carefully' further reinforces Levertov's concern with completing the task to the best of her ability rather than being concerned about the well-being of the patients.

Links to Ways of Thinking

'The Malice of Innocence' shows how ways of thinking can be impacted by institutions whether they be government or corporate bodies. Levertov shows how institutional paradigms can become infectious and morally corrupt. The following of these paradigms can adversely affect vision resulting in insensitivity to the suffering of others.

Levertov highlights how, in order to feel a sense of success and achievement in a large institution, focus shifts to working hard, being dedicated, ordered, disciplined and obedient. But Levertov becomes aware that being single-mindedly devoted to achieving success in each of these areas can come at a cost. The cost is having personal responsibility and human compassion suppressed and she recalls a time in her youth when it happened to her.

Levertov feels that we should not become single-minded in our pursuit of success (and our ways of thinking) as it will lead to insensitivity, heartlessness and a lack of balance. Levertov believes that we can only function successfully in a global world when we are whole and there is a constant interplay of all human faculties; when our priorities are right. If we reduce ourselves to only following a few values, our humanity, compassion and sense of being may well be destroyed. Ironically, large, global organisations demand systems and schedules to run effectively and efficiently. These are presented here as the counter model to responding emotionally to an individual's needs. Levertov believes that insensitivity can be 'paralleled to the way in which scientists have abdicated humane responsibility in the name of pure or objective research'.

Questions

1. "A glimpsed world"..."the story moved on into the streets". What story is referenced in the above quotation?

2. Why did the speaker not follow the "story" but rather, "got lost in the death rooms a while."

3. Find an example of oxymoron and describe its effect. Find and example of synecdoche and explain its effect.

4. As a young nurse, what did the speaker both love and hate to do? Support your answer with textual references.

5. Did responding to routine take precedence for the young nurse over responding to humanity? Justify your response.

6. Comment on the effect of the metaphor, alliteration, temporal references and rhetorical question found towards the end of the poem.

7. How do you see Levertov exploring issues which are linked to the concept of Navigating the Global, within this poem?

'A Place of Kindness' From *The Freeing of the Dust 1975* ©1975

Synopsis

In this poem Levertov imagines there to be a figure in a room who is unaware of the violence in the world. She presents the global as containing corruptive forces. She longs for a place that is free from globalisation's homogenisation, economic paradigms, cunning, violence and associated atrocities. Different ways of thinking fail to enable the individual to see the truth and to comprehend this new world full of horrors. The local is presented as 'dumb', illiterate and simplistic, a haven of ignorance. Whereas, the globalised world is capable of violence and atrocities, despite learning and intellect. It has knowledge but not wisdom. The poet implies that the horror of the 20th century has been 'devised' and honed by those in power. A tone of sarcasm and bitterness dominates the text. There is a contrast between ignorance or innocence, and perpetration. The only hopeful idea in the poem refers to the imagination, which enables humans to make sense of the ever-shifting boundaries of our modern world, be they moral, philosophical, geographical or political.

Significant quotes

- 'a dull room/where someone slow is moving/stumbling'

- 'sit there patiently/ doing nothing but be'

- 'Dull/ illiterate saint'

- 'never imagining/ the atrocious skills his kin/ devise and use'

- 'avidly, viciously active/ refining quality'

- 'increasing quantity –/ million by million –/ of standardised Agony Inflictors'

- 'someone dumb…unknown to cruelty'

Techniques and references

The title is a metaphor which refers to an imagined place, or setting where kindness can exist. Levertov appeals to the reader's sensibilities and imagination by proposing that there must be such a place where kindness is present, in spite of all the horror in the world.

The opening stanza ambiguously begins with the abstract noun locator, 'Somewhere,' connoting uncertainty that such a place even exists. When considering the title, the reader expects this place to contain kindness, an abstract idea in itself. However, the 'somewhere' mentioned is in fact just 'a dull room'. This appears ironic as kindness usually implies positivity, warmth and vibrancy. Levertov employs a sarcastic tone, as kindness must appear to be uninteresting and unnoticed by the global forces in her era. The room is devoid of colour to seem less appealing to the audience. Levertov implies that if this place is not enticing, then it will escape the inevitable commodification or homogenisation that other more 'interesting' places have fallen prey to, like countries that have been exploited for economic gain.

The person contained within the room is also ambiguously described as 'someone', further emphasising the otherness of the place, as if kindness is an alien concept at the present time. The persona is described as 'slow' and 'moving/ stumbling from door to chair.' Their movement is accentuated by the sibilance and indirect verb, connoting that the direction is unclear. This person cannot move with any great sense of purpose and Levertov indicates that to navigate in a world of harsh chaos, the individual cannot move decisively.

Levertov further describes the individual in the poem as static and accepting. All that is required is to 'sit there patiently/ doing nothing but be.' This heightened state of bliss is seemingly incongruous in a faced-paced world of success and industry. The alliterative plosive 'b' emphasises the joy that can be found in simply existing in a sheltered room, albeit a dull room, where the individual can enjoy the simple pleasures of life. The room now becomes a place of 'quiet and warmth' where the persona can be 'pleased with the gradual/ slope of day's light'. The visual imagery of the sun setting gradually reinforces the slow pace of life one can adopt, away from the rest of the world's chaos. Here there is time for appreciation of nature's cycles.

The persona in the poem is a male and Levertov implies that he is saint-like, but naïve and simplistic. Utilising appellation, Levertov names him as a "Dull/ illiterate saint" to highlight the humility of saint-like figures in history or religious narratives, who sacrifice themselves for the good of humankind. Here, the saint does not save but exists in blissful ignorance, away from the horrors of the world. His naivety is reinforced as he is unaware of 'the atrocious skills his kin/ devise and use'. The euphemism of their 'skill' also reveals Levertov's biting tone, positioning her as critical of the current political paradigm existing in the era of the poem's publication. She accuses such powers as devising and using their skill and ingenuity to inflict pain. To be knowing and literate may equate to being complicit and rather than a "Dull/ Illiterate saint" we would be faced with a sinner. In this counter image, readers may see themselves.

The inevitable desensitisation that comes with globalised warfare is inherent in the fifth stanza, as Levertov attacks the politicians or warmongers as "Agony-Inflicters". The capitalisation and appellation condemns their actions, as they are seen to be fuelled by greed, success, efficiency and standardisation. Killing has become a process, seen in the phrase, "avidly, viciously active/ refining quality, increasing quantity-/ million/by million- of standardised Agony Inflicters." The cumulative listing of adverbs increases the pace and rhythm of the lines and the parenthetical dashes emphasise the number of people who are at the mercy of these "Agony Inflicters". The matter-of-fact tone employed further highlights the desensitisation; causing pain has become a business in the global world.

Levertov proposes that in this world of horror, there could be a place of kindness, but to believe in such a place, humans must use their imaginations to escape. She contemplates, 'Imagination could put forth/ gentle feelers there.' It is here that Levertov offers some kind of hope. The imagination becomes an abstract yet animated being, almost alien, with 'feelers' to guide the way to a more ethical way of thinking. However, the ability to choose to act, by using one's imagination to find a place away from harm is not certain, displayed by the auxiliary verb 'could'. It is just a hypothetical suggestion.

The final stanza returns to the ambiguity of the imagined place of kindness. Levertov employs a pleading tone, "somewhere there must be/ such a room", imploring the reader to adopt a more critical and imaginative way of thinking.

Links to ways of thinking

The local in the poem is positioned as a place of simplicity and respite from the harsh, uncaring global. The individual existing within the room or place of kindness, retreats from the globalised world as it is too dangerous. Levertov bitterly presents the notion that ignorance could better than the knowledge and experience of reality, which is controlled by agony. A sense of resignation emerges, that economic progress ultimately leads to destruction of compassion and humanity. Levertov offers that to avoid such atrocities, one must adopt a simpler way of thinking and of living, reverting to a basic existence where one can enjoy watching the setting sun in a quiet place. Levertov acknowledges that humans need hope and imagination, created by mythos (myths and stories). They should not just exist with logos (logic or reason) as this may lead to homogenisation and a lack of humanity.

Questions

1. This poem has the imaginative power and whimsical tone of a Michael Leunig cartoon. Explore some Leunig cartoons on kindness or man's treatment of their fellow man. Explore how both composers share similar values and views on Navigating the Global as evidenced through their compositions.

2. What is the effect of the words, "Somewhere" and "Someone" in the first stanza?

3. What contrast is established in the fourth stanza and how is it achieved?

4. What do you imagine " Agony-Inflicters" to be. Why is this compound word capitalised?

5. What does the word "guile" mean?

6. Comment on the effect of the personification in Stanza Seven.

7. How do you see Levertov exploring issues which are linked to the concept of Navigating the Global, or Texts and Ways of Thinking, within this poem?

'The Life of Others', From *Poems 1972–1982 © 1978*

Synopsis

The speaker watches geese flying south in formation, and reflects on man's insignificance and seemingly purposeless existence. The birds fly freely and in group formation connoting unity. Man, however, is presented as oppressed and without a clear direction as he 'crawls' repetitively, 'about and about'.

Significant Quotes

- 'as if in prayer's unison'.

- '…given over/utterly to belief'

- 'convergence toward the point of grace.'

- 'over men who suppose earth is man's.

- 'We humans/are smaller than they.'

- '…and crawl/unnoticed,/about and about.'

Techniques and References

Levertov's use of free verse and couplet form in the first part of this poem suggests the fluidity and freedom of the geese. This changes in Stanza Three where the poem visually captures the convergence of the birds through its structural formation. The line placement shifts to the middle of the page, mimicking the flight of the geese and visually mirrors the "arrow" of the flock's "convergence". This asserts the poet's power of words and form and her ability to control our interpretation of the poem.

The poem, however, opens with the seemingly incongruent image, "Their high-pitched baying/ as if in prayer's unison. Geese honk, rather than bay. The opening word, "Their" is ambiguous but the word "baying" suggests a pack of wolves or dogs, howling in unison as seen in the simile, "as if in prayer's unison". Yet, if the opening word refers to the geese, consider the inverted visual V shaped image of a wolf's upturned snout, howling, baying at the moon. This image transfers to and mirrors the V shape of the united flight of the geese, just as the following stanzas word image does. The sound of baying is high pitched but consider the image visually rather than auditorily. If the auditory pitch is transferred to the sky and the flight, it reinforces Levertov's image of the migrating birds, seeking to escape the cold of winter.

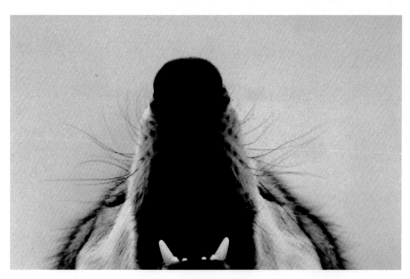

Similarly, "as if in Prayer's unison" can physically link to the unity of the flight formation as the physical shape of the skein's flight mirrors the shape of hands, united in the position of prayer. Thus, on a variety of levels and through multi sensory imagery, Levertov reinforces the image of the migratory birds' journey.

The geese escape the approaching physical and possibly metaphorical winter, the winter of warfare, the polluted cities, "the smoky map", by flying south. "We", the rest of humanity, smaller, less remote than the leaders and the geese are limited to the earth where we, "crawl/ unnoticed,/ about and about the smoky map". Unlike the skein of geese whose unbroken voyage seeks refuge, humanity is reduced to a life of seeming futility. To "crawl" suggests a limited action and to crawl "unnoticed" reflects man's insignificance.

Levertov deliberately manipulates the poem's form to enhance meaning and metaphorically restore nature for the local community. The emphasis is placed on forward and upward movement as seen through the lines 'hierarchic arrow of its convergence toward/ the point...'. The poem is made up of two sentences. The first outlines the movement of the geese and is continuous for six stanzas. This lengthy sentence structurally rides and drifts, "swinging and rippling" like the flight of the birds. In contrast, the second sentence, discussing the humans, is short and concise. This could symbolise just how much humanity has become restricted and rendered insignificant under its current ideology. Nature, "golden earth," by comparison, is free and limitless. Levertov's contrast of these two sentences visually promotes the power and freedom of the natural world over man's transience, confinement and self-delusion as humans, "suppose/ earth is man's" while facing ultimate destruction, possibly through nuclear weapons.

The title, 'The Life of Others' creates a contrast between the constricted life of man and the freedom of the birds. It also highlights how individuals experience globalisation in different ways.

To return to the opening of the poem, 'prayer's unison/' could also be read as an invocation of nature as a way of connecting with past tradition and ritual in order to give meaning to the present. The birds gain spiritual nourishment from each other, as they are united in purpose. For humans, the global space is limitless but not comforting and so the individual maintains the desire to return home, a notion we share with nature. The 'skein of geese/voyag[ing] south' shows the migratory nature of the birds who seasonally navigate this journey through their primal internal compass – an ability which humans have lost as they 'crawl/ unnoticed,/about and about...'. The repetition of 'about and about' emphasises humanity's lack of direction and is a damning depiction of our purposelessness.

Levertov's description of the geese 'swinging and rippling, ribbon tail/ of a kite, loftily...' utilises assonance and metaphor to imply the lightness and weightlessness of the flight for the birds. Furthermore, the metaphor of a kite suggests a playfulness and beauty in the movement of the birds. The present participles 'swinging' and 'rippling' enhance the birds' lack of restriction.

Levertov creates a more sinister tone when referring to mankind. She criticises man's desire to oppress and control the earth in the phrase 'men who suppose/earth is man's.' The possessive apostrophe further reinforces man's desire for power and their adherence to an economic paradigm. Levertov contrasts the bird's freedom with man's need to measure and control nature. Levertov personifies the 'golden earth/ preparing itself/for night and winter,' in order to show the earth's splendour and self-reliance. She then contrasts it with the declining 'night and winter' to suggest the destructive power of globalisation.

The poem ends with a depiction of man, insect like, 'crawl[ing]/ unnoticed'. The verb 'crawling' as well as the adjective 'unnoticed' suggest that mankind has been reduced to a dehumanised state unable to connect with one another. It is reminiscent of Shakespeare's *King Lear,* Act 1, Sc 1, where, Lear can, "/ Unburdened crawl toward death". The poem ends with the image of a 'smoky map'. The noun 'map' implies man's territorial desires and resounds with the war of the era as well as the wars of the past. The land that man has historically warred over is marked by history and history is marked by violence and savagery. The 'smoky' atmosphere suggests not only literally nuclear warfare but also metaphorically suggests man's moral blindness. Smoke is associated with fire and fire can also connote hell. We are left with destructive associations of man's actions.

Therefore, Levertov implies that mankind needs to rise above smoky map of the land like the geese and gain a different perspective in order to change ways of thinking. The repetition of the preposition "over" as in "over lakes", and "over men" highlights the birds' physical and perhaps even moral pre-eminence. The birds unite in their purpose, to prepare for the oncoming winter. It is a didactic message.

Links to Ways of Thinking

Levertov suggests to responders that the only way in which we can navigate the global successfully is to unite and to revert to religious and philosophical ways of thinking. Levertov values the freedom and fluidity of the geese and their lack of distraction in reaching 'a point of grace'. The birds' faith in each other offers them spiritual nourishment and gives them strength to transcend the physical world. For humans, this would involve attaining a meaningful co-existence and the ability to navigate purposefully, together. Levertov is critical of humanity, specifically of those who have chosen to remain passive and of those whose purpose is driven by economic paradigms. She sees the outcome being the control and oppression of others. Levertov conveys a message. Be willing to adopt new perspectives and simplify ways of thinking by looking into nature in order to re-assess ourselves. She offers a bleak image of humanity floundering in a blind haze of corruption where the individual does not have the capability to navigate successfully.

Questions

1. In what ways is a skein of geese like a pack of canines baying and "prayer's unison"?

2. What is the effect of the words,

3. What contrast is established in the fourth stanza and how is it achieved?

4. What do you imagine "Agony-Inflicters" to be. Why is this compound word capitalised?

5. What does the word "guile" mean?

6. Comment on the effect of the personification in Stanza Seven.

7. How do you see Levertov exploring issues which are linked to the concept of Navigating the Global, or Texts and Ways of Thinking, within this poem?

'What It Could Be', From *Poems 1972–1982 © 1975*

Synopsis

Levertov is distraught and outraged by the environmental destruction being caused by the mining of uranium. She was concerned by her contemporary society's ways of thinking which valued power, industry and money over protection of the natural environment. Over forty years later, her words seem to take on a predictive and preternatural quality.

The exploration for uranium started at the end of World War II as a result of the military and civilian demand for uranium. Uranium is used to build military weapons and nuclear power plants. It is also a relatively scarce resource, although Australia is one country that has reserves.

Levertov respects the ancient people who were aware of the power of mother earth but who did not feel the need to excavate and possess what lay within her. On the other hand, Levertov is disgusted by her contemporaries who mine for power and money. She feels that they insensitively tear up the earth in order to possess uranium for the purpose of controlling and destroying others. Levertov's message is to leave nature alone. In doing so humanity will prove its righteousness, reverence and love. Not mining uranium will show that humanity has risen above torture, violence, murder, power and greed.

Significant Quotes

- 'lies always under/the most sacred lands–Australia/Africa/America'

- 'wherever it's found is found an oppressed/ancient people who knew/long before white men found and named it/that there under their feet..../lay a great power.'

- 'And they knew the folly/of wresting, wrestling, ravaging from the earth'

- 'Now, now, now at this instant,/men are gouging lumps of that power,'

- 'Breaking the doors/of her sanctum, tearing the secret/out of her flesh.'

- 'showing forth /the human power/*not* to kill, to choose/not to kill:'

- 'the sign/providing witness,/occasion,/ritual/for the continuing act...

- *non*violence, of passionate/reverence, active love.'

Techniques and references

Levertov structures the poem's subject into two distinct sections. The first half of the poem is about the ancient people's respect towards mother earth whilst the second half is about Levertov's contemporaries who torture and destroy the land. These two sections provide a contrast to each other. The first half incorporates natural imagery; 'rock', 'mountain', 'watersprings' whilst the second half uses violent imagery, 'gouging', 'tortured', 'breaking', 'tearing,' to contrast past and present values and ways of thinking towards the land.

The opening clearly delineates uranium as a source 'with which we know/ only how to destroy'. The syntax inversion foregrounds the subject of the poem and its heavy and debilitating presence on humanity. Levertov uses the superlative 'most' to show how uranium has always existed under these precious '... most sacred lands-/Australia, Africa, America'. The listing of the three continents, coupled with their multi-syllabic sounds affirms the vastness and richness of the lands, whilst the tricolonic listing creates a chant-like tone creating a sacred, spiritual atmosphere.

Levertov reminds us of the ancient people who were 'oppressed' yet knew,

> 'long before white men found and named it/that there under
> their feet..../lay a great power.'

She holds the ancient people in high esteem as even though they did not have the technological advances of her contemporaries, they chose to respect the land instead of seeking to improve their own 'oppressed' conditions. The ancient people were aware of the 'folly/of wresting, wrestling, ravaging from the earth'. Here Levertov cleverly uses the repeated 'r' sound and a tricolonic listing of powerful verbs to show how obstinate and determined we are in our ways to extract from the earth. We will try every manoeuvre until we get our way. In light of nuclear reactor meltdowns in the years since her poem was written, Levertov's warnings take on added wisdom.

The tone changes in the second half of the poem. Levertov sounds frustrated, desperate and disappointed. This can be seen through the repeated 'Now, now, now at this instant,/men are gouging lumps of that power.' The repetition of the present tense heightens the intensity and urgency that something must be done to stop man's mining at this very moment. The verb gouging further suggests man's greed and carelessness when plundering earth's treasures. Contemporary man's ways of thinking are violent and destructive. Levertov describes man's quest to unearth the uranium as 'Breaking the doors/of her sanctum, tearing the secret/out of her flesh.' Here harsh plosives coupled with the present participle heighten the sense that this action is taking place here and now. The earth is personified as a sacred and holy woman who is being forcefully invaded.

Levertov heralds another change in tone with the conjunction 'But' when stating that if we left the uranium in the earth its 'true force' in years to come would be to show man's righteousness. Her approach is now much softer as she tries to persuasively convince her audience that it would be a marker and symbol of man's ability *not* to kill, to choose/not to kill:' if we stopped mining. The repetition of 'kill' coupled with the italic 'not' and verb 'choose' reminds the audience that they are in control and can in fact put an end to the mining if they choose to do so.

Finally, Levertov reminds responders of the ways of thinking that should be embraced in order to navigate our world successfully and in harmony with Mother Nature. Leaving the uranium unmined would be a sign that provided 'witness,/occasion,/ritual/for the continuing act of /nonviolence, of passionate/reverence, active love.' Here the listing heightens the importance of these values to humanity. The visual indentation of witness/occasion/ritual metaphorically shows how far removed we have become from these traditional markers of local existence. The final adjectives 'passionate' and 'active' remind us that we should all take responsibility for what is happening to the earth. It reminds us that we should care instead of remaining passive and accepting government and corporate mining.

Links to Ways of Thinking

Levertov's 'What it Could Be' sends out a message to humanity to change their ways of thinking. Whilst the globalised world has made positive advances in terms of technology and discovering new forms of energy, it has also brought along with it environmental destruction and a new cause for fear. Levertov feels that the global world's scientific and economic paradigms have indoctrinated people's mind-set. Humanity has come to value ease, comfort, efficiency and cost instead of protecting the future of the environment.

Nuclear power is more powerful and efficient than any other source. It is reliable and cheap. However, Levertov feels the catastrophic impact that this will have on the future of our world will far outweigh its immediate and temporary benefits. Levertov wants her contemporaries to respect Mother Earth and value its power rather than destroy it.

She urges humanity to leave its selfish and greedy ways of thinking behind and reminds them of the torture, murder and violence that they inflict on the earth and, as a consequence, onto themselves. Levertov urges her audience to embrace a new way of thinking (or rather an ancient way of thinking), which is to practise nonviolence, respect and love towards Mother Earth. She feels that these actions will filter into the way humanity treats one another and so will promote a forward progression and a harmonious navigation of our global world.

Questions

1. How does Levertov contrast the values of a nations' first people towards their land and the attitude others?

2. Why is uranium described as a "great power"? You may need to research uranium.

3. What is the "it" in the title referring to?

4. How might uranium be seen as a symbol? Support your answer with close textual reference.

5. How do you see Levertov exploring issues which are linked to the concept of Navigating the Global, or Texts and Ways of Thinking, within this poem?

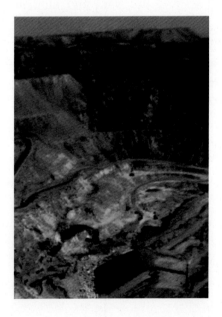

'Talk in the Dark' From *Candles in Babylon* © 1982

Synopsis

The poem is a conversation outlining the loss of opportunity in the wake of nuclear warfare. Levertov imagines a world lacking in purpose and direction and where individuals live in a constant state of fear. The voices in the poem discuss fear, loss and death. They reference the Hiroshima explosion and predict a bleak future for humanity if this scale of violence is to continue. The poem serves as a didactic warning for humanity to cease such violent actions in an increasingly globalised world.

Significant quotes

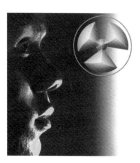

- 'We live in history'

- 'We're flies on the hide of Leviathan'

- 'Now it's to be a mass death'

- 'How can we live in this fear?'

- '...but where can I live /if the world is gone?'

Techniques and references

The use of free verse and mostly couplet form metaphorically represents the fragmentation of the individual in a globalised world. Repeated use of questioning at the end of the poem reinforces the fact that, at present, there is no solution or comfort offered for the individual. At this stage they are alone in their navigation. It is worth noting that Levertov's later poems are more assured, following her conversion to Christianity, in 1984. In the centre of the poem the structure shifts from couplets to tercets (3 lines) when describing mass death. This increase in stanza length emphasises the perpetuation of mass violence throughout history as the speaker recognises its 'nothing new'. It also visually connotes the increase in fear and paranoia for the individual.

The title 'Talk in the Dark' utilises the verb 'talk' to show how the only action available to individuals is muted conversation held in fear. The darkness symbolises a lack of knowledge as well as the dark evil of the nuclear age. Images of dark, nuclear winters are also associated with the title. The speakers are in the metaphorical dark of the fear of nuclear attack and face the prospect of oblivion.

The opening line 'We live in history, says one', is suggestive of humanity's passivity in a period of constant change.' This is shown through the collective pronoun 'we' as well as Levertov's use of the present tense, highlighting the implication, that we as individuals must take action in order for there to be change. Levertov's 'says one' foregrounds the fact that we have become faceless, anonymous and detached from one another. This is ironic as there is an implication that there is unity in the opening word of the first line, however, by the time the line finishes we realise that there is a lack of communal cohesion.

The second line of the couplet, 'we're flies on the hide of Leviathan, says another,' uses the metaphor of Leviathan, a mythical beast, as a symbol of globalisation. Humans have been reduced to insignificant insects, surviving only in a pitiful state as humanity becomes ever more decayed.

The idea of mass death and mass graves is depicted in the line 'Now it's to be a mass death.' The adverb 'now' adds a sense of immediacy yet establishes a tone of resignation in accepting the impending doom that will come as a result of nuclear warfare. The speaker seems to have some knowledge that 'Mass graves… are nothing new' which suggests that humanity has always been accepting of this cycle of violence and this has resulted in the decay of societal values. The repetition of 'mass' heightens the scale of disaster that is to come.

The shift from present tense to future in '…but this time there'll be no graves,/all the dead will lie where they fall,' connotes this disastrous fate that will befall humanity as a result of their acceptance of this ideology. The high modality in 'all the dead will lie where they fall' is the only certainty that humanity can count on in this fragmented and chaotic post modern world.

The question 'How can we live in this fear?' presents the immediacy of life for the individual and the limitations imposed on the individual by adhering to this anxious way of thinking. There is a tone of helplessness and anguish inherent within this question. Levertov's voice emerges here and confronts the reader. Her purpose is clearly to question the ways in which humanity operates and whether this is a sustainable and meaningful way to navigate an increasingly dangerous, global world. The only solution offered is to live 'From day to day'. However, Levertov still find this limiting response dissatisfying as it will continue to isolate the individual as can be seen through the repeated phrases on 'says one' and 'says another' throughout the poem.

The final couplet 'I want to live, says another, but where can I live/if the world is gone?' reflects man's primal instinct for survival and necessity of having a place or space in which to live. Levertov's use of the conjunction 'if' offers a glimmer of hope for humanity as this way of thinking has not yet been fixed and man still has the ability to change this way of thinking. However, ending on a question causes ambiguity and leaves the reader feeling uneasy about the future. Levertov shifts from her opening inclusive pronoun 'we' to the exclusive pronoun 'I' to show the need for individual action and accountability in changing ways of thinking.

Links to Ways of Thinking

'Talk in the Dark' explores the fear and paranoia of nuclear threat in a globalised world which endorses economic and scientific paradigms. In 1982, when the poem was published, there was worldwide knowledge that the global powers held in excess of fifty thousand nuclear weapons which could destroy the planet. Levertov's poem exposes the terror faced by individuals in an increasingly globalised world where violence is greeted with violence. There is an inherent lack of faith and stability witnessed in this post modern world. A focus is given to individual, rather than collective, identity and this is expressed through the detached voices which represent individual identity. Levertov presents a fragmented world, devoid of religion and philosophy, lacking in culture and ritual; a world where people are on the brink of being lost. This total decimation of humanity reflects the ever-shifting boundaries of the global world, resulting in unrest and dissolution on a mass scale. Levertov challenges the reader to change their ways of thinking towards violence and war. She suggests that an individual in a post modern epoch can only successfully navigate their global world by working in unity instead of isolation and through valuing collective benefits based on survival of the planet over personal motives based on economic paradigms.

Questions

1. How does Levertov 's poetry reflect the climate of fear that permeated the Cold War era?

2. Why is this considered a didactic poem?.

3. What is the "Dark" in the title referring to?

4. How are paradigms reflected in this poem?

5. How do you see Levertov exploring issues which are linked to the concept of Navigating the Global, or Texts and Ways of Thinking, within this poem?

SUGGESTED RELATED TEXTS

Fiction

- *Behind the Beautiful Forevers* – Katherine Boo (2012). Also a **play** of the same name by David Hare (2014)

- *Battle Hymn of the Tiger Mother* – Amy Chua (2011)

- *Inheritance of Loss* – Kiran Desai (2006)

- *The Poisonwood Bible* – Barbara Kingsolver(1998)

- *The Namesake* – Jhumpa Lahiri (2003)

- *The Shipping News* – Annie Proulx (1998)

- *Shantaram* – Gregory David Roberts (2003)

- *The God of Small Things* – Arundhati Roy (1997)

- *White Teeth* – Zadie Smith (2002)

- *The Mosquito Coast* - Paul Theroux (1981)- Consider pairing this with Kingsolver's text. Theroux' novel has been made into a film (1986). Edwards, in The New York Times, Feb 14th, 1982, praises Theroux' text, concluding "It is, ...a remarkable comic portrait of minds and cultures at cross-purposes"... These words are also relevant to aspects of Kingsolver's novel.

- **Short Stories by:**

- Rana Dasgupta

- Jhumpa Lahiri

- Alastair MacLeod

- Haruki Murukami
- Lavanya Sankaram
- Tim Winton

Films

- *What the Bleep Do We Know* William Arntz, Betsy Chasse, Mark Vicente (2004)
- BBC Documentary - *Last Whites Of The East End* (2016)
- *The Joneses* Derrick Borte (2009)
- *Trainspotting* Danny Boyle (1996)
- *Syriana* Stephen Gaghan (2005)
- *Brick Lane* Sarah Gavron (2007)
- *An Inconvenient Truth* Al Gore (2006)
- *Independent America* Hanson Hosein (2005)
- *Babel* Alejandro González Iñárritu (2006)
- *Children of Heaven* Majid Majidi (1997)
- *Bowling For Columbine* Michael Moore (2002)
- *The Cup* Khyentse Norbu (1999)
- *The Descendants* Alexander Payne (2011)
- *Up in the Air* Jason Reitman (2009)
- *Blood Diamond* Edward Zwick (2009)

Non-Fiction Texts

- *Wrong About Japan* – Peter Carey (2004)
- *The World Is Flat: A Brief History of the Twenty-First Century*- Thomas L. Friedman (2006)
- *The Lexus and The Olive Tree* – Thomas Friedman (1999)
- *The Global Soul: Jet Lag, Shopping Malls, and the Search for Home* - Pico Iyer (2001)
- *Affluenza* – Oliver James (2007)
- *No Logo* – Naomi Klein (2002)
- *The City: A Global History* (Modern Library Chronicles #21) – Joel Kotkin (2006)
- *The Collapse of Globalism* – J Raulston Saul (2005)
- *Fast Food Nation* – Eric Schlosser (2003)
- *Globalisation and its Discontents* – Joseph Steiglitz (2002)
- *Making Globalisation Work* – Joseph Steiglitz (2006)
- *Ripped and Torn: Levi's, Latin America and the Blue Jean Dream* – Amaranta Wright (2006)

Picture Books

- *When the Wind Blows* – Raymond Briggs (1982)
- *Flight* – N Wheatley and Armin Greder (2015)

MODEL ESSAY

Read the question below carefully and examine the essay outline on the following pages. Try to develop your essay along these lines.

A Note on Essay Writing

The essay is the main form of written response to a question or hypothesis in the field of the humanities: literature, history, philosophy and so on. You will write many essays in your career as a student in secondary school, and you may write many more in university. Essays are regarded as a conventional form of response, allowing for the evaluation of a piece of work according to prescribed principles, and permitting the assessment of the work in relation to other works embodying the same principles. Simply put, therefore, there are *rules* to writing essays. Essays have a degree of formalism, and you will spend time in class before the HSC discussing the form of a good essay.

Rules or principles, however, do not equate with a neat and easily accessed *formula*. An essay that is *formulaic* may be passable but would not demonstrate the inventiveness and critical thought that is merited by a very high mark.

A strong essay is formed *around* an argument, a response to a question. It will present a clear point of view, perspective and critical thinking, supported with close textual analysis. Content and structure is important. The best essays are not draped over a predetermined and rigid structure with a few quotes thrown in. Therefore, point number one, before beginning to write, plan and *have something to say*. Two, before beginning, consider whether what you have to say is *worth saying:* is your argument the product of careful and critical thought, sustained analysis, close and repeated readings of the text? The HSC exam questions will require moulding of your thinking to suit syllabus requirements and rubric outlines as well as shaping responses to specific questions. But, your thought processes and knowledge of the texts and module should be intact *before* you sit the exam. You should be an authority on the *subject,* not the essay form. Of course, to be authoritative in both areas is a bonus!

Three: *your argument is your own.* Scholarly work is always undertaken to provide a unique and individual insight into an area of study. If what you are saying is not unique and individual to you, it is not worth saying. Scholarly work is about commenting on a history of ideas from a unique *perspective* while maintaining an awareness of that history. If original thought were not the point, there would be no such thing as research institutions, universities, scholarly works and essays.

Four: master the basic craft of essay writing. You will be asked to write an introduction, body and conclusion. The introduction should be a point of entry into your argument, nothing more. It should be clear, concise and formal in tone. The body should be a close analysis, revealing a complex and sophisticated understanding of the module and elective– as well as a close, nuanced reading of the texts set for study. Every sentence should advance your argument. Quoting should be brief, relevant and discussed only in terms of the argument. Your conclusion should not be a functional summary of what has preceded it. Rather, it should be a provocative culmination of a subtle argument.

A few practical tips

i.   Take five minutes to plan your essay. The 'moulding' of your ideas takes place here. Therefore, take the full five minutes. Consider the question in detail: what does it ask of you? You may find it helpful to consider 'keywords' in the question.

ii. Merge your knowledge of the topic with the question – HSC examiners reward answers that respond to their questions. Prepare an answer to the question in one minute. Use points to structure the introduction (stating the line of argument) body and conclusion.

iii. Assess your response to the question. Does it account for the subtleties of the question? Every question has levels of meaning – every question is as complex as your approach to it permits. Does your response engage with the question in a subtle, complex and sophisticated way? Does it incorporate the module, elective and rubric?

iv. Will the strength of your argument – and the originality of your critical thought – be reflected in the structure you have planned prior to writing the essay?

v.   Start writing.

Question

In Navigating the Global, composers not only confront the dilemmas of globalisation but respond to their times. Discuss

(N.b. **Two prescribed** texts are referenced in the following response.)

Sample essay:

In Navigating the Global, composers not only confront the dilemmas of globalisation, through theme, contrasting settings and characterisation but they also manipulate textual forms and features and tone in response to their post modern times. Composers highlight the negative consequences of valuing modern economic paradigms over the environmental and spiritual and, in so doing, challenge responders. Levertov manipulates poetic form and features in 'The Sun Going Down Upon Our Wrath' (1972) to explore the dilemma of choice in our increasingly violent world. She questions whether there is a choice for humanity to adopt a different way of thinking. In 'The Life of Others'(1978) Levertov presents the dilemma between existing individuality or adopting a collective way of thinking. She continues to manipulate textual form by employing a fragmented poetic style, indicating the initial disorder of her era. The audience is positioned to consider the powerful control of mankind over nature and the destructive impact that this has on the individual. In Annie Proulx's 1996 novel *The Shipping News*, the author utilises the novel form to confront the dilemmas associated with living in a globalised world, such as shaping an individual identity and forming meaningful relationships. Sofia Copolla's text *Lost in Translation* (2003) utilises the filmic form to explore the dilemma of making personal and cultural connections in an increasingly chaotic post modern epoch.

Levertov manipulates poetic form and feature in 'The Sun Going Down Upon Our Wrath' to explore the dilemma of choice in an increasingly violent world. She questions whether there is a choice for humanity to adopt a different way of thinking to successfully navigate the globalised world. Levertov warns the audience that once knowledge is gained, innocence and beauty will fade. She employs the subjunctive 'if' in the phrase, 'if you are warned will your beauty/ scale off, to leave/ gaping meat livid with revulsion?' to highlight that it is a choice resting with the audience, to change their way of thinking and choose to learn about the truth of war and economic exploitation. The cost of learning this truth however, is revealed as Levertov suggests that this knowledge will strip the knower of their beauty or innocence, to reveal 'gaping meat livid with revulsion' beneath.

Graphic imagery reflects her own disgust at people's ignorance, and she reduces such humans to 'meat', items or commodities to be slain by global warfare. The poem ends with a final question and unease in changing existing ways of thinking, as she states 'could there be/ a reversal I cannot hoist myself enough/ to see,/ plunge myself deep enough/ to know?' Here, Levertov experiences her own internal dilemma as she questions her own ability to see the truth and challenge her own ways of thinking. Knowledge is revealed to be a deep well or pool of truth into which she must plunge. It is a difficult decision as the laboured verbs 'hoist' and 'plunge' connote the challenge of this task. Her final question leads to uncertainty and fear, which is furthered with the conditional tense 'could'. This ambiguity shows the reader that in our post modern world there is no certainty and hence her dilemma will be ongoing as it is difficult to step outside one's own context to be an objective observer.

Levertov structures this poem using irregular line lengths and stanzas, enjambment and caesura, to create a sense of internal chaos and uncertainty about the future. This is furthered by the lack of rhyme as the comfort that comes with uniformity or patterns is no longer available to the speaker or the audience.

In 'The Life of Others' Levertov's presents the dilemma of individuality versus collective thinking through a manipulation of textual form. The audience is positioned to consider the powerful control of mankind over nature and the destructive impact that this has on the individual. Levertov creates a sinister tone when referring to mankind's individual greed. She criticises man's desire to oppress and control the earth in the phrase 'men who suppose/earth is man's.' The possessive apostrophe further reinforces man's desire for power and their adherence towards an economic paradigm. The poem ends in a depiction of man as insect like 'crawl[ing]/unnoticed'. The verb crawling as well as the adjective 'unnoticed' suggest that mankind has been reduced to a dehumanised state unable to connect with one another due to their individualistic values.

However, Levertov's answer to this dilemma is to present the beauty of collective unity. The opening line of the poem 'Their high pitched baying/as if in prayer's unison/remote,' invokes nature as a way of connecting with past tradition and ritual in order to give meaning to the present. The reference to 'prayer' suggests the spiritual nourishment gained from unity in sound and purpose. For humans, the global space is limitless but not comforting and so the individual maintains the desire to return home, a notion we share with nature.

The 'skein of geese/voyag[ing] south' shows the migratory nature of the birds who seasonally navigate this journey through their primal internal compass- an ability which humans have lost as they 'crawl/ unnoticed,/about and about...'. The repetition of 'about and about' emphasises humanity's lack of direction and is a damning depiction of our purposelessness. Levertov's description of the geese 'swinging and rippling, ribbon tail/ of a kite, loftily...' utilises assonance to imply the lightness and weightlessness of the flight for the birds. Furthermore the metaphor of a kite suggests a playfulness and beauty in the movement of the birds. The present participles in 'swinging' and 'rippling' enhance their lack of restriction.

Levertov's use of free verse and couplet form in the first part of this poem suggests the fluidity and freedom of the geese. This changes in Stanza Three where the poem visually captures the convergence of the birds through its structural formation. The line placement shifts to the middle of the page, mimicking the flight of the geese. This asserts the poet's power on the written page and her ability to control our interpretation of the poem. Levertov deliberately manipulates the form to enhance meaning and metaphorically restore nature for the local community. Hence Levertov, explores the dilemmas of globalisation through poetic features and form. Notions of fear, control, lack of choice and conflict and the opposites of unity and freedom, arise from a Cold War and Vietnam War context.

In Annie Proulx's *The Shipping News*, Proulx utilises literary features to confront the dilemmas associated with living in a globalised world such as shaping an individual identity and forming meaningful relationships. Proulx's use of characterisation highlights the inability to communicate face to face. This can be seen through the protagonist Quoyle's broken relationship with his parents. This is evidenced the repeated depersonalised nouns, "The father, diagnosed with liver cancer... the father dictated, the mother typed a suicide note." A dilemma of the globalised world is that Quoyle cannot form meaningful relationships even with those with whom he is supposed to be closest. The detached tone clearly illustrates Quoyle's broken family ties. Furthermore, the answering machine on which his parents leave their suicide note reflects the replacement of human connection with technology. Quoyle's sense of isolation is further reinforced through the rhetorical questioning in, "What was left for him in Mockingburg?" coupled with asyndeton, "Unemployed, wife gone, parents deceased." The dilemma facing Quoyle is that he has nothing, which is seemingly common in the modern, global world. However, Proulx chooses to solve the dilemma for her protagonist by enabling his assimilation into the local community of Killick-Claw, allowing him to, "experience moments in all colours." The synaesthetic imagery shows how one becomes whole when they are able to form meaningful relationship as well as an identity.

Through his strong relationship with Wavey, which can be seen through the listing and sensual imagery when berry picking 'she fell, or he pulled her down. They rolled over the massed cushions of berry plants, clinging, they rolled, hot arms and legs, berries and leaves, mouths...', Quoyle is able to find a sense of self. However, the local provides Quoyle with an identity as seen through the addition of the initials 'R.G' on his editorial page. Therefore Proulx manipulates features to show the dilemmas of a globalised world.

Sofia Coppola's *Lost in Translation* utilises the filmic form to explore the dilemma of making personal and cultural connections in an increasingly chaotic post modern epoch. Coppola utilises characterisation show the alienation of her protagonists. Charlotte's despondent tone, as she speaks to her sister on the phone after having visited a temple in, "(she) didn't feel anything" establishes her inability to connect to an unfamiliar environment which promised spiritual nourishment.

Similarly, the close-up of Bob's bewildered face as his business associates bow in greeting, suggests that he also fails to connect with others, a dilemma facing the individual in the post modern era. Yet, Coppola admits the opportunities and positive economic impacts that globalisation brings to individuals through the relationship that Bob and Charlotte form through isolation. Their instinctual connection is depicted at the end of the film through the inter textual reference to Casablanca's final dramatic farewell scene, symbolic of the end of a relationship. However, for Bob and Charlotte there is a sense of hope. This is established through the close-up of Charlotte's smile at the end of the film as she walks away from her embrace with Bob.

Furthermore, their intimacy is heightened through Bob's inaudible whisper into her ear. This makes it a private moment that the audience is not privy to and hence highlights their ability to connect despite their previous dilemma of feeling isolated in a post modern, chaotic world.

When Navigating the Global, composers not only confront the dilemmas of globalisation but also manipulate textual forms and features in response to their times. Through so doing, they highlight the damage, both personal and social, wrought by globalisation's focus on economic paradigms and the restorative power of adopting new models. Levertov manipulates poetic form and features in 'The Sun Going Down Upon Our Wrath' to explore the dilemma of choice in our increasingly violent world. She questions whether there is a choice for humanity to adopt a different way of thinking. In 'The Life of Others' Levertov presents the dilemma of individuality versus collective thinking through a manipulation of textual form. The audience is positioned to consider the powerful control of mankind over nature and the destructive impact that this has on the individual. In Annie Proulx's *The Shipping News*, Proulx utilises the novel form to confront the dilemmas associated with living in a globalised world such as shaping an individual identity and forming meaningful relationships. Sofia Copolla's *Lost in Translation* utilises the filmic form to explore the dilemma of making personal and cultural connections in an increasingly chaotic post modern epoch. All three composers draw on, respond to and raise fears, problems and issues arising from their post modern times.

Evaluate this essay.

1. Does it have a clear and relevant structure?

2. Does it answer the question?

3. Is there adequate textual referencing throughout and is it used appropriately?

4. Are enough poetic, narrative and filmic techniques incorporated? If not, explain.

SAMPLE ESSAY QUESTIONS

To what extent do contextual perspectives shape expectations about work and home in the elective Navigating the Global?

In your response, refer to TWO prescribed texts and at least TWO related texts of your own choosing.

Texts in this module are all related to a particular context and offer differing attitudes regarding Navigating the Global.

To what extent does this statement reflect your study of this module? In your response refer to TWO prescribed texts from the elective you have studied and at least two texts of your own choosing.

In the elective, Navigating the Global, composers blend their chosen form with content which reflects conflict.

Evaluate this statement with reference to TWO prescribed texts AND texts of your own choosing.

Significant texts possess an enduring relevance and invariably raise issues of context and values.

Write an essay in which you evaluate the significance of TWO prescribed texts AND TWO texts of your own choosing.

Destiny is affected by context, fate and choice.

Discuss this idea with relation to the elective, Navigating the Global. In your response, refer to TWO prescribed texts AND TWO texts of your own choosing.

Navigating the Global involves the concept of transformation. Transformation, however, may be viewed from different perspectives. Some will desire and achieve transformation, some will desire and strive for it, yet never achieve it while others will consider and reject the notion.

Consider this statement in relation to TWO prescribed texts AND at least TWO texts of your own choosing.

The notion of the status quo is not well aligned to Navigating the Global.

Discuss with reference to TWO prescribed texts AND ONE related.

When composers and characters are concerned with Navigating the Global, responders are often confronted with value clashes.

Evaluate the validity of this statement with close reference to TWO prescribed texts AND TWO related texts.

Navigating the Global involves personal choices and public trends.

Evaluate the extent to which these thoughts express ways of thinking in this elective, and how these ways of thinking are shaped in texts.

In your response, refer to TWO prescribed texts AND other texts of your own choosing.

SAMPLE IMAGINATIVE RESPONSE QUESTIONS

Compose a narrative which incorporates new interactions and new possibilities between the local and the global.

Navigating the Global in a post modern world,means juggling the global and local and evaluating one's values. Explore this idea in a piece of imaginative writing.

Write three descriptive paragraphs in which you explore the rhythm of a traditional, local setting. Contrast these with three descriptive paragraphs in which the rhythm of the global is explored. Research your settings thoroughly prior to writing.

Compose a piece of creative work in which locally and globally related paradigms are shown as conflicting.

Write a feature article which illustrates local customs giving way to global aspects of production.

The modern age is marked by contrasts - fear and confidence, hope and hopelessness, wealth and poverty, tradition and change. Take one of these pairings and explore it creatively, in relation to your module and elective. You may write in any form you wish.

Write a narrative, in letter or email form, exploring some of the choices which are inherent in a Navigation of the Global.

Compose a speech to a teenage audience which is designed to be didactic and motivational. It must draw on Levertov's poetry for inspiration and address aspects of the module and elective's rubric.

REFERENCES

Also consider - http://www.boardofstudies.nsw.edu.au/hsc_exams/

http://www.thefreelibrary.com/%22The+art+of+the+octopus%22%3A+the+maturation+of+Denise+Levertov's...-a020846964

'On The Malice of Innocence Poetry in the Classroom Author(s)': Denise Levertov Source: *The American Poetry Review,* Vol. 1, No. 1 (Nov.-Dec. 1972), p. 44 Published by: American Poetry Review Stable, University of Illinois Press : Urbana, Chicago, and Springfield.

Greene, Dana, *Denise Levertov: a poet's life.* Somerville, Massachusetts, 1974.

The Mystical/Political poetry of Denise Levertov. Nielsen, Dorothy. The University of Western Ontario (Canada), ProQuest, UMI Dissertations Publishing, 1991. NN71996.

Bonnycastle, Stephen *In Search of Authority* – Third Edition: *An Introductory Guide to Literary Theory* – 2007. Chapter four. 'Paradigms and Paradigm Change.'